Education

and the

Global Concern

Other Titles of related interest

HUSEN AND POSTLETHWAITE
International Encyclopedia of Education: Research and Studies

HUSEN AND POSTLETHWAITE
The International Encyclopedia of Education: Supplementary
Volume One

POSTLETHWAITE
The Encyclopedia of Comparative Education and National
Systems of Education

TITMUS
Lifelong Education for Adults: An International Handbook

FAGERLIND AND SAHA
Education and National Development 2nd Edition

Education

and the

Global Concern

by

TORSTEN HUSÉN
University of Stockholm, Sweden

PERGAMON PRESS
Member of Maxwell Macmillan Pergamon Publishing Corporation

OXFORD · NEW YORK · BEIJING · FRANKFURT
SÃO PAULO · SYDNEY · TOKYO · TORONTO

U.K.	Pergamon Press plc, Headington Hill Hall, Oxford OX3 0BW, England
U.S.A.	Pergamon Press, Inc., Maxwell House, Fairview Park, Elmsford, New York 10523, U.S.A.
PEOPLE'S REPUBLIC OF CHINA	Pergamon Press, Room 4037, Qianmen Hotel, Beijing, People's Republic of China
FEDERAL REPUBLIC OF GERMANY	Pergamon Press GmbH, Hammerweg 6, D-6242 Kronberg, Federal Republic of Germany
BRAZIL	Pergamon Editora Ltda, Rua Eça de Queiros, 346, CEP 04011, Paraiso, São Paulo, Brazil
AUSTRALIA	Pergamon Press (Australia) Pty Ltd., P.O. Box 544, Potts Point, NSW 2011, Australia
JAPAN	Pergamon Press, 5th Floor, Matsuoka Central Building, 1-7-1 Nishishinjuku, Shinjuku-ku, Tokyo 160, Japan
CANADA	Pergamon Press Canada Ltd., Suite No 271, 253 College Street, Toronto, Ontario, Canada M5T 1R5

First edition 1990

Library of Congress Cataloging in Publication Data
Husén, Torsten, 1916–
Education and the global concern/by Torsten Husén. – 1st ed.
p. cm.
1. Educational sociology. I. Title.
LC189.H88   1990 370.19–dc20   90–32518

British Library Cataloguing in Publication Data
Husén, Torsten, 1916–
Education and the global concern.
1. Education
I. Title
370
ISBN0–08–040489–8

Printed in Great Britain by BPCC Wheatons Ltd., Exeter

Contents

Preface

MY INTERESTS as a researcher in education have since the early 1970s focussed on the school as an institution and its problems in a modern, highly industrialized, society where formal education has become an increasingly important asset in the life career of the individual and the economic development of society at large. I have been studying the problems the school has been facing and how they are related to lack of compatibility with other institutions in society, particularly the family.

The external framework of formal schooling has over the last few decades rapidly changed. It has become considerably prolonged, and the structure of basic schooling has, in a double sense, become comprehensive. It caters to children from all walks of life in a given area and offers all its curricular programs under the same roof. But changes and innovations affecting the framework have by and large left the content of schooling unaffected: the curricula and—above all—the methods of teaching.

Over a long career as a social scientist I have taken particular interest in studying educational change and innovation, how such processes are initiated and the role played by research.

The essays included in this book were chosen for their relevance to the areas of interest mentioned above. The first part of the book aims to 'take stock' by identifying the problems and describing their setting. The second part takes up the role of research and what it can achieve—and not achieve. The emphasis here is on the compatibility between the 'paradigms' and the aims of that research. A distinction is made between policy-oriented research and research aimed at the needs of the classroom practitioners.

The third part discusses strategies of educational reform, in particular their social and political ramifications. Some pedagogical problems are also dealt with in a discussion of what modern educational technology can do.

The readership I have in mind for this book consists, of course, of educators, particularly those who take a special interest in the conditions of their field of work and study. I also hope that the book will serve as a reader for students of education preparing themselves for the classroom and that it may help to widen their horizon beyond pure pedagogy. The latter being important in its own right, the teacher candidate also needs to view the classroom problems in their broader context, which in our time has not only national but international dimensions as well.

Stockholm, September, 1989   T. HUSÉN

Introduction

THE ESSAYS in this book have all been written since the mid-1980s. But they reflect, as mentioned in the Preface, interests and preoccupations which have absorbed me over a longer period. They also reflect how the perspectives of my scholarly endeavors have widened. Education as a practical pursuit tends to be rather provincial, not to say local. The typical educator in the field is after all faced with children here and now. International co-operation and communication has, however, in a few decades widened his horizon enormously. Typically, comparative education as a clear-cut speciality had its breakthrough around 1960 at a time when most colonial empires disintegrated and new nation-states, for which education played an important role in building national identity, began to emerge.

The present collection reflects the interests and activities of an academic who for more than forty years has been preoccupied by educational research and reform both in his home country, Sweden, and in other parts of the world. Although structural changes which made provision for greater equality of opportunity was the top priority, it was also clear that one had to study in depth how the school curriculum could be reshaped so as to prepare young people for a society in flux. Rapid urbanization, high occupational mobility and a shift towards a highly technological society was bound to have strong repercussions on education.

In 1961 I published a collection of papers, some of which were originally prepared for the 1957 Swedish School Committee, under the title *Schooling in a Changing Society*. The overriding idea behind my thinking about the new curriculum, given the rapid economic and social change, was that specific areas of competence (as defined by school textbooks) were bound to become rapidly obsolete. Therefore, the main emphasis in the curriculum should be on equipping the students with the basic skills for a broad range of largely unforeseen situations. Traditional formal schooling acquired during the early part of life was no longer enough to prepare the individual for coping with the complex and changing exigencies of modern society. We would have to envisage a system of 'life-long' or 'recurrent' education which would help the individual to meet the demands of adult life better than the limited fare provided by the basic school. These ideas were later spelled out in my book *The Learning Society* (1974).

In conducting studies leading up to these publications I became increasingly convinced that the school as an institution in modern industrial and high technology society had to be subjected to critical scrutiny. Failures of the school to meet the needs of an increasingly achievement-oriented society were dealt with in my book *The School In Question* (1979). Some years later my thinking about the school in modern society was brought together in *The Learning Society Revisited* (1986).

In the late 1950s—under the auspices of the UNESCO Institute for Education in Hamburg—I became involved in cross-national evaluations of national systems of education. These efforts became institutionalized as the *International Association for the Evaluation of Educational Achievement* (IEA) whose Chairman I was for sixteen years. At the core of the IEA research stood the quality of education.

Having spent almost my entire career in educational research it was time for me to evaluate its role and conditions, epistemological and others. After the Second World War education was conceived as the main vehicle for economic and social development, particularly in the Third World. Educational planning became a centerpiece in the development strategy. I had the privilege to serve on the Committee which prepared the establishment of the *International Institute for Educational Planning* in Paris and served for a decade as Chairman of its Governing Board. Given the perspective I gained in that role as well as Chairman of IEA, and as Director of the Institute for International Education at the University of Stockholm, I became interested in building research competence, particularly in developing countries in the process of planning and building national systems of education.

In recent years I have studied the role of research as related to policy-making and classroom practices. Some of these studies were reported in *Educational Research and Policy: How Do They Relate?* (1984) co-edited with Maurice Kogan. This relationship is much more problematic than the one between the natural sciences and physical technology. Educational research as a separate field of inquiry developed later than other fields of research. It draws heavily on the social sciences which were already drawing on the paradigms of the natural sciences at the end of the nineteenth century. Therefore, it was expected that educational research would be able to bring about improvements in school practices equal to the improvements that the natural sciences, via technology, were contributing to in industry, for instance. The gap between expectations and promises on the one hand and actual performance on the other led to frustrations, not least among the practitioners, and sparked in recent years a debate on the proper role of educational research. This debate in its turn has inspired a controversy on the adequacy of the prevailing positivist research paradigms in education. An epistemological debate emerged.

A central issue dealt with at some length in this book under the overriding theme of 'Reform' is the problem of 'global learning' which, in a way, is an extension of another, perennial and overriding issue in modern education, that of general versus vocational education. 'Global' is conceived here with a double meaning. It has to do with substantive issues central to mankind and relevant to the entire world. They are in that sense 'global.' But the teaching and learning about these problems as well as about all major issues has to be conducted in a global way, that is to say, by integrating perspectives and specific pieces of knowledge from many different traditional disciplines. 'Global learning' is a way of trying to overcome the fragmentation that comes from the rapid specialization of research as well as of vocational training in all fields.

The development of the content of education has been strongly affected by the intrinsic development of the historically given disciplines which constitute school subjects. Specialization, as well as the enormous output of new knowledge generated by scientific research, has made the cognitive landscape increasingly fragmented, multifaceted and difficult to comprehend. The overriding problem for curriculum planners, not least at undergraduate level, is how to ensure intellectual coherence in what is taught. This modern, complex and highly technological society needs not only specialists for its extremely diversified functions but also 'generalists', people who can 'put it all together'. This is the background for my preoccupation with 'global learning', an expression originally coined by the former Rector of the United Nations University, Soedjatmoko.

Acknowledgments

I WANT to express my gratitude for the permission to reproduce original or revised versions of articles which have appeared in the UNESCO *Courier* (May 1983); the *Oxford Review of Education* (Vol. 13:23, 1987; and Vol. 14:3, 1988; *Interchange* (Vol. 19:1 and Vol. 19:3–4, 1988); *Phi Delta Kappan* (February 1985); and *Fundación Santillana* (Conference report in Spanish, 1987).

1

Taking Stock

Milestones to the Learning Society (1983)[1]
Secondary School in Modern Society: A 'Disaster Area'? (1984)[2]
Young Adults in Modern Society: Changing Status and Values (1984)[3]
Integration of General and Vocational Education: An International Perspective (1988)[4]
Observations on a Future-Oriented Education (1986)[5]

Introduction

HAVING DEVOTED half a century to education and educational research, I have tried to 'take stock.'[6] This exercise has been conducted in several essays with a double perspective, both a retrospective and a prospective one. The first essay in the thesis section is an attempt to identify 'milestones' in the development of education since the mid-nineteenth century. This was a period when institutional schooling in the industrial countries became universal, first at the primary and then, much later, at the secondary level. Desperate attempts have, in recent decades, been made in developing countries to universalize primary education against considerable demographic and economic odds. In the rich countries 'continuing' and/or 'recurrent' education became part of the adult life pattern in rapidly changing economies. In trying to cope with the 'enrollment explosion' in the 1960s, high hopes were attached to new educational technologies. But the school is, by its very nature, a highly labor-intensive 'industry' and new technologies have not been labor-saving.

There is a growing realization that the school as an institution today is beset by problems which will become even more difficult tomorrow, problems which have to be conceived and dealt with in the context of society at large. The school is not operating in a vacuum. Problems can

1

not be resolved solely by bringing about changes in the structure and practice of the school in isolation. They have to be tackled as social problems, not least by bringing other institutions, such as the family, into the picture.

To be young in the modern society is in several respects something fundamentally new. Formal schooling has been prolonged. Preparation for tasks shouldered in working life and to become fully-fledged workers takes more time. There is a period after what was previously regarded as adolescence when young people tend to be 'superfluous.' A new stage in life, 'young adulthood,' has important implications for the educational system.

Striking a proper balance between general and vocational education has been a central and pervasive issue in the debate on reforms of secondary education. The main point in the chapter on this topic is that the best vocational education is a solid general education. The realization of this has, in most countries, led to a postponement of vocation-specific subjects and topics in the school curricula.

Notes

[1]Published in the UNESCO *Courier*, May 1983 (in some 20 languages) pp. 13–18.

[2]Originally presented as a lecture at the University of California, Berkeley, in 1984. An adapted version was published in the February 1985 issue of *Phi Delta Kappan* (pp. 398–402) under the title 'The School in the Achievement-Oriented Society: Crisis and Reform'.

[3]Paper prepared for OECD as part of the OECD/CERI project *Transition to Adulthood*. Part of the material was used for Husén and Coleman, *Becoming Adult in a Changing Society* (Paris: OECD 1985). An adapted version has been published in the *Oxford Review of Education*, Vol. 13:2, 1987, pp. 165–76.

[4]Paper prepared in 1988 for the European Centre for the Development of Vocational Training (CEDEFOP) in Berlin.

[5]Adapted from a paper prepared for the Fundación Santillana, Semana Monographica in December 1986. Published by Fundación Santillana in *Los Objetivos de la Educación*, Madrid 1987, pp. 26–31.

[6]The Royal Swedish Academy of Sciences invited the author to give a lecture in the series '50 years with science.' It was given in the fall of 1987 and published under the title *Femtio år som utbildningsforskare* (Fifty years as an Educational Researcher) in the Academy series *Documenta*, No. 45, March 1988. Another attempt to take stock is an article in the UNESCO journal *Prospects*: No. 3, 1989 p. 351–360, entitled 'Educational Research at the Crossroads.'

1

Milestones to the Learning Society

WHAT CONSTITUTES a 'milestone', or even a 'revolution', in education is, of course, a matter of judgment. Important institutional changes in education do not occur as abruptly as revolutionary upheavals on the political and social scene. Furthermore, it is not always easy to distinguish lasting milestones from ephemeral fads, such as the so-called new mathematics, and only time can tell one from the other. In education we can, however, in retrospect, at certain points in time, identify sequences of events that together constitute a change that over a long period has had a strong impact on the social fabric.

Looking back over a century and a half it appears to me that one could identify five sets of milestones on the road to the learning society of today. The first was the introduction by the mid-nineteenth century of universal primary schooling in the northern hemisphere, when legislation on mandatory schooling was passed in many countries. This occurred mainly during the period 1815 to 1880. Thus, there was some spread between countries.

The second set of milestones marked the gradual introduction of a common basic school, sometimes referred to as a comprehensive school, catering to students from all walks of life in a given area or community. This occurred well into the twentieth century with the Soviet Union and the United States taking the lead and Western Europe trailing behind with a more class-stratified system, particularly for the age range 10–15.

The third set of milestones could be placed after 1960 and indicates the 'enrollment explosion' at all stages in both the industrialized and non-industrialized world. The fourth set signals massive literacy campaigns in Third World countries and a new conception of adult education under labels such as life-long, permanent or recurrent education. A fifth milestone, finally, is represented by the entry of new technology onto the educational scene, something that happened after 1960.

3

There were certain socio-economic, ideological and political forces behind the legislation on mandatory schooling (either mandatory attendance or mandatory for the communities to set up schools). Important changes occurred in the role of the family in connection with industrialization and the concomitant urbanization. There is no doubt that the need for children to be cared for while parents worked long hours in the factories gave a strong impetus to the provision of schooling. Typically, in several European countries, in rural areas where the children's labor at home was needed they attended school only part-time, whereas in the urban areas they went to school full-time. Many farmers were by no means enthusiastic about parliamentary decisions forcing them to send their children to school.

Two new educational institutions emerged in industrialized England during the first part of the nineteenth century: the Bell-Lancaster system for providing elementary schooling (by using more advanced students as tutors) on a massive scale with a minimum of adult teachers, and infant schools for children in the age range 2–7.

A Swedish social statistician who went to England in the early 1830s to study the infant schools recorded his observations in a travel report 'Notes from a Journey to England at the End of the Summer 1834'. The infant schools which were run by philanthropic organizations took care of the small children when their parents were away working. They taught the children certain skills, such as very elementary reading and arithmetic. This was, however, not their main aim. In these schools 'children already from the age of two are getting used to attentiveness, order, obedience, reflection and self-initiated activity.'

When in the 1830s child labor was prohibited or limited by law in Britain, children in the age range 7–12 came into focus, and demands for their schooling began to be voiced. The need for custodial care of children in urban areas was in the interest of several parties, such as parents and owners of enterprises. But it would be a serious mistake to believe that this was the main force behind the introduction of universal elementary schooling. The liberal quest for universal suffrage, for democratic participation in the decision-making process both locally and centrally as well as for greater equality of opportunity was also an important motive for establishing a universal elementary school.

During the decade after the Second World War, largely under the prompting of UNESCO, mass literacy teaching became a prime task in Third World countries. In spite of the fact that universal primary education was proclaimed a top priority for educational policy, for instance at the meeting of African Ministers of Education in Addis Ababa in 1960, the most striking feature of educational efforts in the developing countries has been the massive literacy campaigns. They are, with the exception of the Soviet Union, without any historical precedent in preliterate Europe.

A characteristic of these campaigns was the attempt to integrate literacy with vocational skills with the aim of helping to improve the economic plight in particular of the small and poor farmers. But, again, as was the case in the attempts to make primary schooling universal, the chief impetus was a strong belief in literacy as the backbone of a functioning democracy with the participation of enlightened citizens.

The demand in Europe and North America for a common school for children from all kinds of homes can be traced back to the time when legislation was enacted introducing universal primary schooling for 'the people'. Typically, the elementary school established by law at various points in time in some European countries was for the next century referred to as the 'people's school' (*Volksschule*, *folkskola*).

It was a school that reflected a highly class-stratified society. Different types of schools for the various social strata were in most quarters taken for granted. For a teachers' conference in 1881 a Swedish conservative educator, teaching in the classical *gymnasium*, published a brochure entitled 'What Direction Should a Reform of Our Schools Take?'. The overriding idea was that each of the three main social classes should have the type of school that corresponded to its 'needs.' The general elementary ('people's') school was meant for the 'working classes and the lower classes of artisans.' The grammar school was for the upper class. What was now needed was a third type of school for the middle class of skilled artisans, business men and farmers. The three types of school should run parallel to each other without any organizational connections.

Two years later in deliberate criticism of this a young elementary school teacher, Fridtjuv Berg, who some twenty years later became Minister of Education, published a brochure called 'The Elementary School as the Basic School' in which he advocated a basic school which would cater to children from all walks of life.

Comprehensive versus a stratified and selective education was a major issue in European public policy in the years following the Second World War. The word 'comprehensive' denoted from the outset a secondary school which ideally served all the students from a given area under the same roof and offered all types of program, both academic and vocational. In Europe, with its traditionally segregated school structure, the comprehensive school was advocated as a replacement for the socially and academically selective school. The breakthrough for a comprehensive conception of schooling in Europe came after 1960.

Enrollment statistics in the twentieth century relating to secondary and higher education show certain striking features. In the northern hemisphere, well into the middle of the century, formal education beyond a minimum (compulsory) primary schooling was the prerogative of a small social élite, although there was a limited flow of academically gifted young people from the lower classes to schools which prepared pupils for the universities as well as to the universities themselves. But by and large the industrialized countries were still what sociologists call ascriptive societies, where social status is more or less determined at birth.

By the mid-twentieth century the enrollment pattern had changed dramatically in both industrialized and non-industrialized countries. Both types of countries experienced what has often been referred to as an 'enrollment explosion.' Since the turn of the century enrollment in post-primary education in most industrialized countries increased in a linear fashion. This had been the case with elementary education in the preceding century. But since 1950 the growth in secondary and higher enrollment in these countries has, to express it in mathematical terms, been exponential. There are countries in which the number of students doubled or even quadrupled in less than ten years. Similar patterns of growth have occurred in Third World countries but they apply there to *all* stages of the educational spectrum.

Equality of opportunity has become a major objective for educational policy in countries all over the world. It is a growing concern as the employment system tends more and more to use formal education as the first criterion of selection among job seekers and as educational achievements increasingly determine social status. The expansion of the number of places in further education has led to an increase in both the absolute and relative number of young people of lower class background who have won access to upper secondary and higher education. It appears that social background plays a less powerful role in educational attainments in non-industrialized than in industrialized countries. This has been an important factor in the expansion of post-primary education in the developing countries.

Many developing countries have experienced an almost explosive increase in secondary school enrollment. The financial implications have been serious for poor countries running schools mainly on public funds and with a population structure dominated by young people.

The social structure of the enrollment has, as indicated above, tended to become more balanced than in the highly industrialized countries, and this in turn has made formal education an even more powerful vehicle of social mobility. In other words, formal education is playing a central role in an increasingly meritocratic society. Educated intelligence tends in our days to become the substitute for social origin and inherited wealth. No wonder, then, that formal education is regarded as an almost endless ladder up which one should try to climb as high as possible. No stage or level of the system tends to have a goal or profile of its own. It is regarded merely as a step to the next level.

Young people are keenly aware that formal credentials in terms of schooling are not only strategic in their life careers but constitute the first criterion of selection among those who enter the job market. They are aware that unemployment among those with a minimum of formal education is much higher than among those with more advanced education. There is much talk about the 'educated unemployed,' but the fact is that, all over the world, they find it much more easy to obtain employment than those with a minimum of education. The employment statistics show that their unemployment rate is much lower.

A fourth milestone on the way to the learning society of today was recently passed almost unnoticed: this was a mushrooming growth of various forms of adult education, not least the sudden increase in many countries of adults 'going back to school.' It appears that the breakthrough in the industrial countries occurred around 1970. Enrollment in formal schooling at the upper secondary and the university level, which previously had rarely included adults who had already embarked on their working life, suddenly exploded. This process was facilitated by legislation on the right to leave of absence for educational purposes and by financial support, for instance, from pay-roll taxes.

The rise of adult participation in formal education is largely a phenomenon limited to the more advanced industrial countries where until recently adult education, often under the aegis of various popular movements, was dominated by evening classes or study circles. Education is now closely woven into the career web of the individual in societies where the occupational structure and the requirements for efficient job performance continuously change as technology changes.

Formal education has always been a labor-intensive enterprise. The insatiable demand for teachers, particularly in developing countries, has been a serious bottleneck which has tended to stifle the expansion of school education. No wonder, then, that hopes ran high about what the new educational technology would be able to achieve.

In the developing countries radio and television were in the early 1960s seen as the answer to the teacher shortage. In addition, other forms of technology, such as programmed learning and teaching machines, were considered in the more affluent parts of the world. Distance teaching, particularly by means of radio, proved to have a strong impact in Third World countries suffering under the 'tyranny of distance,' but it has also been a godsend in sparsely populated areas, such as parts of Australia. A breakthrough in the new technology was triggered in 1947 by the invention of the transistor. Within a few years it revolutionized electronic equipment and brought the small, portable radio within the reach of almost everybody.

The most recent development in educational technology, that might eventually revolutionize education, is represented by the mini-computer.

All technological devices used in education so far have shared the drawback of allowing only for one-way communication. You cannot talk back to a TV-screen or a teaching machine. The computer, however, allows student feedback and two-way communication, and the student can thus interact with the computer, both in programming and in the actual learning situation; this affords him ample scope for creativity and this in turn stimulates his motivation to learn.

Computer-based instruction remained an exclusive amenity of affluent societies and their schools as long as the equipment used in the individual school or classroom had to be connected with a computation centre with its big and expensive machinery. But as computers have become increasingly compact and prices have gone down, they have begun to be within the means of the less affluent countries. When and to what extent they will be financially accessible to students in poorer countries only time will tell. But considering how quickly and unexpectedly pocket calculators have made their entry on the educational scene there is reason to believe that this will occur fairly soon.

2

Secondary School in Modern Society: A 'Disaster Area'?

Introductory Observations

THERE SEEMS to be a common recognition that the school—particularly the secondary school in highly industrialized societies—has become a troubled institution. Whether or not we are entitled to speak about a 'crisis' is a matter of taste and judgment. When asked about the US secondary school at an OECD meeting in the early 1980s, an Assistant Commissioner of Education referred to it as a 'disaster area.'

There are, indeed, certain indicators that objectively and quite unequivocally point to a 'malaise.' Absenteeism, vandalism and turnover of teaching staff have soared in many countries over the last few decades. Attitude surveys, such as the ones conducted by the International Association for the Evaluation of Educational Achievement (IEA), (Walker, 1976; Husén, 1979), show that a high proportion of young people in the age range 13–16 tend to dislike school. Part of the 'malaise,' as perceived by the general public, has to do with frustrations about what a reformed and progressively more expensive school designed to serve all of the students was expected to achieve and what it actually has achieved. In many countries the school was expected to provide educational programs that would equally well serve both the academically and vocationally-oriented students. It was expected to make a highly significant contribution to citizenship education in a society where the role of the family has gradually been reduced. But the discrepancy between rhetoric and reality has become strikingly large.

Given the array of troublesome symptoms and the wish to improve the school as an institution, can we arrive at a diagnosis about which we can agree before proceeding to propose some reforms? We have begun to realize that some kind of 'incrementalism,' that is to say, doing more of the same things—for instance, making more funds available—will not significantly improve the situation. In some instances it would even make the situation worse.

It seems to me that any attempt to arrive at a deeper diagnosis of today's problems has to start from the following two overriding points of view:

(1) Schooling has increasingly become the main vehicle for achieving status and making a successful career in working life, that is to say, modern society has become increasingly *meritocratic*.

This system of sorting and sifting according to schooling has strong repercussions on what goes on in the school. Marks, tests and examinations become the main preoccupation among the majority of students, particularly among those who are more successful. In this scramble for credentials, which begins at an early stage, there are early winners and losers depending upon the background and the support children are able to enlist on the part of the home.

First and foremost, the main repercussion is that learning to a large extent is motivated by external and not by internal rewards. B. F. Skinner has given us a brilliant illustration of the difference between the two categories of rewards. 'An American student, who in flawless French can say, "Please pass me the salt," gets an A. A French student saying the same gets the salt.'

(2) Schooling, as has been the case in other fields of public administration, has increasingly become *bureaucratized* and formalized, which reflects a tendency to conceive of it in terms of a product-oriented, manufacturing industry.

It would, indeed, take me too far if I tried here to spell out in detail the symptoms of the 'malaise' and how I have arrived at a diagnosis subsumed under the two headings: meritocracy and bureaucratization. I shall therefore confine myself to the more conspicuous symptoms and to a discussion of how they are interrelated. But before doing so I should like to emphasize that the meritocratic and bureaucratic syndromes are closely connected. Increased credentialism enhances bureaucratic formalism and vice versa. You could also say that both are inimical to an innovative spirit and flexibility, which are basic prerequisites for the genuine purpose of school education, namely, to 'train the mind' (Sizer, 1984). There are certain tendencies in our modern, highly technological meritocratic society which are at cross-purposes with basic values in education to which quite a lot of lip-service is paid.

Schooling a 'Processing Industry'

Formal schooling has increasingly tended to become a processing industry with the elements of bureaucratization and formalism that go with such an industry. Schooling in this respect tends to develop along the same lines as institutionalized health care. The school was at an early stage an outgrowth and an agent of the immediate community. It supplemented the education provided at home. The teachers, who were in close contact with the community, regarded themselves as working *in loco parentis*. The school at that stage operated on the principle of a relationship between partners on equal footing, which lent a spirit of closeness and humaneness to its work. But increasingly the school has become an instrument of the state, that is to say, of a corporate actor. The system of schooling in the 'asymmetric society' has become a complex, state or nation-wide enterprise with large districts and big school units with a hierarchy of administration and with a teaching staff selected for and assigned to jobs or positions according to an increasingly elaborate legislation and to rules settled by collective bargaining. The school in the 'asymmetric society' (Coleman, 1981) is indeed vastly different from the one in the time of the small red school houses.

The size of the system and its units has already been pointed out. In all industrialized countries with migration from rural to urban areas, there has been a strong tendency to increase the size of the schools. This applies in particular to secondary schools with their more diversified curricula which call for diversification of teacher competencies and school facilities. One cannot provide a minimum of programs and curricular offerings without increasing the number of specialized teachers and thereby increasing the enrollment of students. The Swedish school reforms of the 1950s and 1960s were accompanied by a radical consolidation of municipalities which were designed to be big enough to secure a sufficient enrollment at the secondary level. Thus a reduction of municipalities from 3,000 to less than 300 took place, which meant that there were school districts in the sparsely populated areas which were the size of a small state.

The sheer size easily leads to a formalization of social contacts and controls in the system. In the small setting where individuals are familiar with each other social control can be exercised in an informal way. Those who break the rules are more easily identified and subjected to social sanctions than in the larger setting. But in the latter an elaborate system of rules and formal proceedings have to replace the informal social control. At the same time size and complexity force the system to become more hierarchical.

Size and formalization of contacts lead to fragmentation of contacts with adults. Instruction is increasingly divided between teachers with specialized competencies. Non-teaching staff, such as nurses, social workers, janitors, cafeteria personnel, and psychologists, in increasing numbers have appeared on the school scene. Different aspects of the individual child are apportioned to various specialists. This also applies to child care in society at large. Various agencies and specialists, jealously guarding their own turfs, are dealing in a disconnected way with the same child. One only needs to observe how problems of delinquency occurring in the school are handled by the police, the school and the social welfare agencies to realize the seriousness of this fragmentation.

A by-product of the development just sketched is the emergence of what I would refer to as a 'client-oriented society.' New public institutions, such as day care centers and youth centers, have emerged and a rapidly growing class of publicly employed people is expected to take care of the citizens from the cradle to the grave. Old institutions, such as the school, have been given greatly widened scope with regard to the tasks they are supposed to perform. New institutions, particularly those taking care of children of pre-school age and the elderly after retirement, have emerged. As pointed out above, the services provided by professional experts have become increasingly specialized with nobody taking care of the 'whole client.' There has been an ensuing fragmentation in terms of both kind and continuity between caretakers and clients in these institutions.

The size of the system, as well as its bureaucratization and fragmentation, runs counter to attempts to create a milieu where *individuals* are educated. At the core of genuine educative efforts is the interaction between the teacher and the pupil, between an adult and a growing person. Teaching is often misconceived as simply being a process of knowledge transmission from the more knowledgeable to the less knowledgeable. But the teacher fulfils the important functions of being at the same time a role model and one who motivates the young person to learn something. One of the consequences of a fragmented caretaking with compartmentalized services is a reluctance on the part of the child to 'invest' in a particular adult person. In a setting with a large enrollment, social control is difficult to exercise. Fragmentation of contacts with adults, for instance, compartmentalization between school and home, leads to inconsistencies of norms and difficulties in socialization. The bigger the discrepancy in norms between home and school the more serious problems of discipline.

The 'client-oriented society' easily becomes a control-oriented society where the step between what is justified by caretaking duties and selfserving convenience and power can become very short. Tasks performed by the caretakers easily develop into a network of elaborate control regulations and measures.

A 'Revolution of Rising Expectations'

In trying to diagnose the 'malaise' that besets secondary school in highly industrialized, urbanized and technological societies, I have so far pointed out the meritocratic and bureaucratization tendencies. A couple of decades ago hopes were running high about what the school as an institution would be able to accomplish in terms of improving conditions of man in a society that already had achieved a high material standard of living and could look forward to further improvements in that respect. Opportunities for prolonged formal education were increased manifold. Secondary education was in a short period made universal. Formal equality of opportunity was expected to lead automatically to equalization of life chances. The school was expected to play a dominant role in the social education of young people, making them better citizens who were more co-operative, mutually understanding, tolerant and willing to participate in the political processes of a democratic society.

But rhetoric and reality in education as well as in other fields of public policy, are not always compatible. On the contrary, the discrepancies between expectations and outcomes with regard to school reforms have given rise to frustrations and soulsearching questions. The vastly increased opportunities for furthergoing education have not considerably reduced differences between social classes in participation rates, even though it has narrowed considerably the gap between rural and urban areas in some countries, partly due to urbanization.

It is, of course, almost impossible to establish criteria according to which we would be able to assess over time how tolerant, how co-operative and how democratically minded students are. The objective indicators we have, such as absenteeism, vandalism, and number of students who are involved in criminal acts, do not seem to signal improvements in social education. School discipline does not seem to have improved. Youth unemployment, which appears to be endemic in our society, has its backwash effects on what is going on in the schools, particularly on those students who fail at an early stage and whose prospects on the job market are very dark.

We have begun to realize that there are unrecognized but nevertheless built-in goal conflicts which have been overlaid by the sweeping rhetoric of reformists. Before pointing at some of these conflicts it would be in order to point out that the frustrations to a considerable extent depend on *unrealistic expectations*. In a way, the school has fallen victim to its obvious and highly spectacular successes. In most highly industrialized and affluent countries secondary school enrollment has over a couple of decades multiplied. Children from lower social strata who earlier for economic reasons were almost barred from furthergoing education do now in many countries not have to overcome economic barriers in order to get access to advanced education. Schools are now much better at taking care of the material welfare of the children by means of such conveniences as school lunches and medical services. The school offers a much broader spectrum of learning opportunities both inside and outside the traditional cognitive domain. The school, no doubt, plays an increasingly important role as a babysitting institution in countries where the majority of mothers with children of school age have gone to work outside the home.

These changes have occurred during a period of rather rapid economic growth, when increased provisions in the welfare and educational areas could be accommodated within an expanding economy. The general public got used to the idea of expanding public obligations in these areas and did not find it remarkable that the unit costs, the cost per student per year, over a decade in many countries went up by 50 to 100 per cent in constant prices. Thus, when the economic squeeze occurred and cutbacks in the order of some 5 to 10 per cent were made, these led to quite a lot of doomsday exhortations and talk about 'a catastrophe' for the educational system.

But there was another frustration that resulted from what I prefer to call the 'revolution of rising expectations.' The widely broadened educational opportunities and the easy access to jobs as well as the realization that advanced education led to high status and well paid jobs strongly boosted the enrollment in further education. Formal education was seen as the important vehicle to good jobs. Both parents and students were well aware of this and that one's place in the line of job seekers was determined mainly by how far up on the educational ladder one had been able to climb. The employment system has increasingly begun to use formal education as the first screening criterion when credentials are scrutinized. (Teichler *et al.*, 1976)

But when jobs which traditionally had been filled by young people began to be scarce and when the economy suffered cutbacks, this led to reduced employment of not very productive youngsters. The expectations of many were frustrated, although the employment rate was still by far much higher among those with a formal education beyond the mandatory minimum than among early dropouts.

Goal Conflicts

It has been pointed out above that during the euphoric period of economic growth, educational expansion and rising levels of expectations, certain goal conflicts went either unrecognized or were simply glossed over. The objectives stated in school legislation or in curricular guidelines had in some countries quite a lot to say about education as an instrument of social change, particularly as an instrument of equalization. A Swedish Minister of Education (Olof Palme) in the late 1960s talked about education as 'spearheading' a better society by democratizing educational opportunities. Things did not, however, work out according to such expectations, and this for various reasons. In the first place, schools are there to impart competencies. Already when children enter school there are some whose background makes it easier for them than for others to absorb what the school tries to instill. Therefore as children move through the grades, individual differences in performance increase. It has been suggested that this can be taken care of by individualized teaching, as epitomized in the concept of Mastery Learning developed by my colleague, Benjamin Bloom (1981), and his students. By giving everybody the time he or she needs, the vast differences in learning outcomes can be reduced, and those who otherwise tend to lag behind can be brought up to the level of the more successful students. This can under favorable circumstances no doubt be achieved with certain skills or topics and by mobilizing ample resources in terms of teacher time. What I am saying by no means reduces the value of the ingenious pedagogical idea of how to bring about mastery learning. But what cannot be controlled by mastery learning techniques relates to factors outside the school, in the first place the home and the amount of support the student can enlist on the part of the parents—if he has any.

The tendency for differences in competence attained to increase as students move through the grades is reinforced by what I have referred to as the meritocratic tendencies in our competence-oriented, highly techno-logical and complex society. The rewards for good achievements in school are not intrinsic but extrinsic: better life chances in terms of better jobs and better pay for jobs which enjoys good status. This is the second obvious goal conflict which one tends to sweep under the rug. How is learning going to become appreciated for its intrinsic values if what comes out of it in the final run is essentially something that determines one's life career?

A third goal conflict relates to equality versus quality. It permeates formal education and the expanded opportunities for it in all countries and all societies. In the Third World one attempts to make elementary education universal by enrolling as many as possible without too much consideration to teacher competence and the availability of learning materials and other facilities. Quantity, that is to say, in this case equality, is bought at the price of quality. In more affluent countries secondary education is made universal in the name of equality which then calls for expanded teacher training and individualized programs and teaching strategies. In the most affluent countries this conflict is most acute at the university level, at the stage when elite higher education is changing to mass education. The rather homogeneous and select group which previously entered the universities is now replaced by a highly diversified army of entrants where individuals differ not only in intellec-tual ability and grounding in the relevant subject areas, but in their interests and motivation as well.

A fourth goal conflict concerns co-operation versus competition. Given the social framework within which the school in modern society operates, students soon become aware that they are continuously evaluated in terms of their achievements, expressed as marks or test and examination scores with the purpose of determining who is going to be admitted to the next level in the system and who in the final run is going to be placed at the head or at the tail of the line of job seekers. Curricular guidelines tend to be flourishing in their rhetoric about fostering co-operation by, for instance, group work and mutual understanding, loyalty and sense of responsibility for those who are not as successful as others. But how can this be achieved in a climate of scrambling for those good marks and examination scores which determine one's career?

What Can We Do in Reforming the School?

It is with considerable hesitation that I set out to discuss what kind of changes are called for, even after having tried hard to diagnose what I have called the 'malaise' of the school today. My hesitation derives from two major circumstances. In the first place, the distance is enormous between blueprints for sweeping reforms and the hard, rigid reality. No wonder that many Swedish teachers, when reading the goals set out in curricular guidelines issued by the government refer to them as 'curricular poetry.' Secondly, reforms confined to the school as an institution are bound to be of limited value, because so many of the problems identified above that beset the school are, in the final analysis, problems that beset modern society at large. Some of these problems are unforeseen side-effects of the changes in the material standard of living that have taken place over the last few decades. Others have their roots in changes that have taken place in the school but which in their turn have been initiated by overall changes in society at large.

Thus, reform proposals in order to achieve an impact would have to affect the social fabric as a whole. Tinkering only with reforms that imply changes more or less exclusively within the classroom is often not very helpful. Nevertheless, reforms that I shall hint at here have to be conceived of in the limited sphere of the school as an institution. Some of these proposals were discussed in the late 1970s at a series of international seminars in Europe and the United States, sponsored by the Aspen Institute for Humanistic Studies. These are spelled out in the last chapter of my book, *The School in Question* (Husén, 1979). Since then I have had ample opportunity to discuss them further, particularly in connection with writing a book on transition to adulthood and the role of the school, with my Chicago colleague James S. Coleman. (Coleman and Husén, 1985)

In discussing possible future changes in the institutional arrangements one should in my view keep the following considerations in mind. Genuine care with full responsibility for the individual has historically been the task of the extended family and the close community. Humane attention could be expected to be exercised in this small setting. But in the modern welfare society there has over a long time been a tendency to allocate care (in the widest sense of the word) to larger and larger units, particularly in education and health care. This easily leads to discontinuities and sometimes direct conflicts between the family and the close community on the one hand and the welfare society with its increasing bureaucracy in charge of caretakers on the other. There is a goal conflict between on the one hand personal service and humane attention and equality of service and participation and influence of the 'client' on the other. The responsibility for the individual child has been split up between various agencies with a heavily reduced responsibility being left with the family. Thus, an overriding problem not only for school policy but for social policy at large in the future is what kind of institutional arrangements can be envisaged so as to take care of the 'whole' child. Has the family that tends to wither away to be replaced by some system of boarding schools, where a consistent educative milieu around the clock can be established? The experiences from the experiments with communes in the West and the kibbutzim in Israel seem to indicate that the nuclear family, in spite of the reductions of some of its traditional functions, still is of essential importance for the upbringing of children.

Given the problems that particularly beset the secondary school of today there is ample reason to ask if it is possible for the school as an institution in a credentialling society to serve young people so as to make them reasonably harmonious, well developed, and participating individuals. Can we conceive of alternatives or functional equivalents to the traditional school? To contemplate 'de-schooling' alternatives would be more than utopian. What could be conceived are rather institutional changes that would reduce the role of the state and restore the responsibility of the community and the family for what the school should do. We need to remind ourselves that once schools were established in order to complement the educative role of the family. There were certain competencies that could more easily and readily be instilled by the school than by the family. Thus most of what is discussed in the following could be subsumed under the general heading 'de-institutionalization.'

Genuine education occurs in small, close communities, such as the family, both the nuclear and the extended one, the neighborhood, the small workplace with its apprentices. In a society with large-scale institutions the life of the individual is from the outset segmented into many roles and influenced by many, often contradictory, forces. Under such circumstances more attention is drawn to superficial qualities, such as the dress, and less to deeper character traits for whose assessment and appreciation continuous close contact is required. This applies not least to the big school units, the 'pedagogical factories' which have emerged in modern urban areas. Any attempt to come to grips with the troubled school of today would have to consider the issue of how to establish more self-directed and self-responsible school units with closer ties to the surrounding community.

Some 'Concrete' Proposals

Again, I should like to repeat what I said about the gap between sweeping reform proposals and the rigid realities of the school, and also to indicate that some of the points made here have been spelled out more fully in *The School in Question* (Husén, 1979).

First, steps should be taken to establish smaller school units, which appears, to say the least, to be a utopian proposal after a period of school construction when in some industrialized countries urban secondary schools with enrollments of more than 1,000 students is more a rule than an exception. In countries with a comprehensive set-up, that is to say, where all the programs and all the students from a catchment area are under the same roof, the size of the school plants is simply a logical outcome of comprehensivization. In order to provide a real choice between programs and electives and what goes with it in terms of specialized teachers and school facilities, the enrollment has to exceed a certain minimum that already constitutes a rather big school. But the drawbacks, not least in terms of social control, can be reduced by trying to establish units within the bigger unit. The 'house' system in British secondary schools is an example of such efforts. Students enrolled in a certain program or at a certain grade level can form a sub-unit.

Second, a redefinition of the role of the teacher is called for. The teacher as a provider of learning opportunities, as motivator and a role model, has traditionally worked at the primary school level with its system of self-contained classrooms where one teacher has been responsible for most of the teaching, although specialists in non-academic subjects successively have begun to enter the scene. The problem of fragmentation dealt with above occurs at the secondary school level where due specialization in the cognitive subjects teachers begin to divide the time between themselves. The problem then becomes how to strike a proper balance between, on the one hand, more continuous and permanent contacts between the student and the teacher and, on the other, competent teaching which cannot be achieved without a certain amount of specialization. As things now stand, students in secondary school often have to deal with a dozen or more teachers during a school week. In the subjects where the teacher has to instill certain competencies in the students he cannot spread himself too thinly. Specialization is required in areas such as mother tongue, science/mathematics, history/social studies, and foreign languages, at any rate in the upper secondary school. At the lower secondary level the teaching spectrum can be somewhat broader, but not very much. There it is possible to have two teachers dividing the responsibility for teaching the entire cognitive field. It is at any rate essential that every student has *one* teacher to whom he or she can relate. Whether or not such a teacher can be referred to as a 'home-room teacher' is of secondary importance.

Third, increased parental participation in school matters with increased contacts between teachers and parents within the framework of a given school class is of utmost importance. Good communication between home and school contributes to better understanding and reduced inconsistencies in terms of norms. This relates particularly to students who come from culturally 'marginal' families, be they immigrant ones or not. One way of enhancing the co-operation between home and school is to involve the parents in various school affairs, all the way from helping to prepare social gatherings to teaching in the classroom.

Fourth, a reappraisal of the role of the school in preparing for adult life is called for. The range of tasks that have been assigned to the school has resulted not only in a lot of so called frills but has increased the fragmentation of what the school is expected to achieve as well. The 'back-to-basics' movement has to be seen as a reaction against the overload of tasks, not least what the school is required to do in terms of social education. The fact that so many young people leave school after ten to twelve years without sufficient mastery of the mother tongue has resulted in demands for concentration on certain basic skills mastered by all.

Fifth, the school has to assume a more active role in the transition process from school to work. In most advanced industrial countries vocational guidance has been added to the tasks the schools are expected to shoulder. Specialized guidance teachers have been added to the school staff.

References

Bloom, B. S. (1981) *All Our Children Learning: A Primer for Parents, Teachers, and Other Educators*. New York: McGraw-Hill.
Bromsjöe, B. (1965) *Sämhallskunskap som skolämne*. (Social Studies as A School Subject). Stockholm: Scandinavian University Books.
Coleman, J. S. (1981) *The Asymmetric Society*. Syracuse: Syracuse University Press.
Coleman, J. S. and Husén, T. (1985) *Becoming Adult in a Changing Society*. Paris: Organisation for Economic Co-operation and Development.
Husén, T. (1979) *The School in Question: A Comparative Study of the School and Its Future in Western Societies*. London and New York: Oxford University Press.
Sizer, T. (1984) *Horace's Compromise*. Boston: Houghton-Mifflin.
Teichler, U. *et al.* (1976) *Hochschulexpansion und Bedarf der Gesellschaft*. Stuttgart: Klett.
Walker, D. (1976) *The IEA Six Subject Survey: An Empirical Study of Education in Twenty-one Countries*. Stockholm and New York: Almqvist and Wiksell and John Wiley (Halsted Press).

3

Young Adults in Modern Society: Changing Status and Values

THERE IS A growing recognition that in modern, highly industrialized societies something *fundamentally new* is occurring with regard to the transition from what traditionally has been conceived as youth to adulthood. It would suffice here to point at the impact of extended schooling, which has brought about a considerable prolongation of the period of dependence on elders, and at the changing character of working life. The majority of young people in most industrial countries a few decades ago left school at 14 to go to work. Now the majority stays in school until 18, and the typical entry jobs have disappeared from the labor market. One fundamental change has to do with the transition from a society where families are the building blocks to a corporate society where the locus of responsibility has been shifted from the individual and his family to impersonal institutions and where individuals are in the position of, and increasingly have become, dependent clients (Coleman, 1981). Under such conditions the fundamental characteristic of adulthood, the assumption of full responsibility for one's own actions, is considerably delayed. We can observe today among 30–40 year olds lifestyles that traditionally have been associated with adolescence and youth.

Important changes have occurred in the conditions determining the criteria for defining adolescence and adulthood and the way transition from the one to the other occurs. Not only is there a prolongation of the preparatory period for adult life represented by formal schooling, but a prolongation of the period between schooling and settling down with a relatively stable job as well. During a long period of 'floundering' various kinds of jobs are tried out. Stable work for a living, which traditionally has been an important ingredient of adult personal identity, has under such circumstances lost its importance.

An important earlier criterion of adulthood, namely marriage, has tended to lose its significance as the habit of co-habitation grows. Formal education as provided by the school system was previously limited to the years before 18–20 years of age. Now a rapidly growing number of adults are taking additional formal education in order to broaden the basis for further vocational training and to enhance their working career. The fact that education has become 'life-long' or 'recurrent' contributes to blur the differences between youth and adulthood.

There is today no well-defined destination guiding the transition from youth to adulthood. Another factor blurring the stages is the combination or alternation between school and work that has emerged among young people in the highly industrial countries since the 1960s. The practice of 'stopping out' for some time, even for some years between lower and upper secondary school or between the latter and postsecondary education, has made 'school-leaving' beyond the mandatory age limit highly flexible and relative.

Changing Conception of Transition to Adulthood

In Stanley Hall's monumental and pioneering study *Adolescence* of 1904 the stage before entering the adult world was conceived as one of 'storm and stress' (*Sturm und Drang*). The expression was once coined by Goethe in *Die Leiden des jungen Werther* in the late eighteenth century and signified the romantic mood as well as opposition seizing on young people vis-à-vis adult society. A similar picture was developed by, for instance, Edward Spranger (1924) who typified his youth in the *Wandervogel* movement.

The next important study of adolescence was that by Charlotte Bühler in Vienna. Her seminal book *Das Seelenleben des Jugendlichen* (1921) was important in two respects. She made a distinction between 'puberty' and 'adolescence,' the first being the period of physiological maturity and the second the *Kulturpubertät*, when the young person achieved the psychological and social maturity required for the culture to which he or she belonged. Her analyses of how young people reacted were based mainly on a selection of diaries kept by the young people themselves. The young people whose diaries were included came from rather sophisticated and articulated intellectual upper or middle class milieux and were not representative of young people in general.

Margaret Mead's (1928) study on 'coming of age' in Samoa relativized the previous conception of adolescence. There was no 'storm and stress' in the 'primitive' society. An important social dimension of adolescent development could be identified. Social anthropologists showed that the dynamics and length of adolescence depended on the cultural setting. In pre-industrial societies the onset of physiological puberty rather abruptly marked a transition to adult responsibilities. There was no extended and 'problematic' period of transition of the kind we have been familiar with in highly industrial and urbanized societies. The transition was symbolically emphasized by initiation rites. The young person was, after a short period of learning and preparation, considered to be ready to support himself, to establish a family of his own and to exercise the religion of his elders. The confirmation rites administered by the Lutheran state church in the rural society where I grew up were remnants of these initiation ceremonies. A salient characteristic of the transition period in the preindustrial society was that it was a *short* one.

Social psychologists and sociologists after the Second World War began to conduct empirical studies of adolescence. The study of 'youth culture' in eight Middle-West high schools in the United States, published in *The Adolescent Society* (1961) by Chicago sociologist James Coleman, was a landmark. It focussed on the value-orientation of young people, to what extent they felt that they adhered to values proclaimed by their parents, their teachers or their peers. The thesis of a separate youth culture and a concomitant 'cleavage' or 'gap' between the young and their elders has since then been challenged as well as validated by replicative studies, for instance by Andersson (1969, 1982) in Sweden.

It was not until the 1960s that there was any mentioning of 'alienation' or 'youth revolt.' The events of the late 1960s, particularly at universities all over the industrialized world, gave rise to grave concerns about the relationship between generations. Keniston's 1968 study on *Youth, Change and Violence* appears to be rather typical of the reactions in the West. Soul-searching efforts were made in trying to explain the 'radicalism' of the young people. But, again, 'young people' in this context, as was once the case when Stanley Hall conducted his investigations, were still represented by an educated elite, mostly young college and university students. When studies of changing values among young people were conducted, it was found that the variability in attitudes and values *within* the youth generation was even larger than between young people and their parents.

By the mid-1970s the focus of concern had shifted from revolt and alienation among young people in educational institutions to unemployment among those who left these institutions early. In spite of the fact that the school enrollments increased considerably, to the extent that the situation was characterized as an 'enrollment explosion,' the unemployment rate in the highly industrial Western societies, particularly among those who left school after completion of a mandatory minimum, remained high and tended to increase.

Doubts were raised about how the school 'prepared' the young people for life. Social problems were increasingly moving into the schools, in particular into the urban schools, and in the early 1970s one began to talk about 'crisis in the classroom' (e.g., Silberman, 1970; Husén, 1979). Certain objective indicators pointed to the existence of undeniable problems, such as increasing student absenteeism, particularly in the secondary schools. In some big city school systems one began to discover that on a typical day up to one fourth or one third of the students in the 13–16 age range were absent. Vandalism had grown and could be measured objectively by the soaring repair bills. Teacher turnover had increased and—in spite of tougher competition in the job market—teacher training institutions are increasingly having difficulties attracting high quality candidates (D. Kerr, 1983). In the United States no fewer than five high-powered commissions, set up by both public and private agencies, took a close look in the 1970s at the problems of secondary schools which have become 'disaster areas' (Passow, 1975).

The basic dilemma facing young people is that reaching physical maturity, which not long ago marked the transition from childhood to adult status, is followed by a long period of semi-adult status before the young person in the early twenties 'settles down' in a somewhat consistent adult role. Criteria of adulthood are now unrelated to physical maturity, which in modern society is reached one to two years earlier than a century ago (Tanner, 1962).

Criteria of adulthood are both formal and non-formal. Legislation defines adult status in many different respects. The problem is that these criteria coincide far from perfectly in time. Adulthood in a juristic sense relates, for instance, to the minimum age of obtaining a driver's licence, conscription for military service, marriage licence, the right to be served alcohol in a restaurant or the right to buy alcohol, the right to vote, and, not least, the minimum age of being legally responsible for economic transactions and subject to sanctions according to the penal code. In most countries the minimum for various prerogatives occurs at different ages, all the way from 14–15 to 20–21.

Informal, but socially crucial, criteria of adulthood are completion of formal education, entering working life on a relatively permanent basis, and having a steady sex partner by marriage or co-habitation. Today among urban youth in highly industrial societies typically about one third to one half of the 20 year olds are still in full-time education. The majority still live with their parents and more than half of them do not have a steady partner. But the years after 20 lead to rather drastic changes in these respects (Andersson, 1982). The majority leave home and begin to set up families of their own. But still at the age of 23 about one fourth to one third have not reached the independent status according to the informal criteria mentioned above.

Andersson (1982) studied how young people in Sweden from 10 to 20 looked upon what adulthood meant. Pre-adolescent children tended to emphasize the power to do whatever one wants to do. To be adult is to be bigger, stronger and more smart than the young. During mid-adolescence adulthood tends to be regarded from the point of view of elders barring the young from getting access to adult prerogatives, adulthood is perceived in terms of power and prerogatives. But at the age of 20 it is mostly perceived in terms of experience, patience and endurance as well as of taking responsibility, planning for the future and achieving independence.

There often appears to be an ambivalence with regard to the adult role among those who have reached young adulthood. Adulthood still exerts a certain lure, not least in terms of material rewards, but on the other hand obtaining adult 'rights' also implies having to shoulder adult responsibilities. In many instances there is a reluctance against entering adulthood with all its demands of accepting things as they are and of living a dreary life dominated by routine. Young children regard adulthood as highly attractive but during adolescence and post-adolescence when they begin to realize what it means to be an adult and they are becoming aware of the insecurity and difficulties of the transition period, they increasingly take a hesitant attitude.

Institutional Changes and Shift of Responsibility for Socialization

In a pre-industrial economy the family is a unit of both production and consumption. Children are integral parts of this joint venture. At an early stage they have to look after younger siblings, watch sheep and cattle, and are assigned simpler tasks in the household. Under such auspices child rearing is part of the productive functions.

In modern, highly technological and urbanized society there is a marked disjunction between learning and production which has fundamental csonsequences for child rearing. The changes are mainly the following:

(1) Production has moved out of the homes to workplaces, factories and offices, with many, highly specialized, jobs. The workplaces are often located far away from where the family resides. The houses where the parents sleep overnight constitute sleeping suburbs.

(2) Both parents are increasingly working (mostly as employees) outside the home. Recent years have in many countries witnessed an explosive increase in the number of working mothers. Two salaries have increasingly become a prerequisite in order to sustain the acquisition and use of certain amenities that are regarded as part of an acceptable standard of living.

(3) The preparation period for adult roles, both as a worker and a citizen at large, has become prolonged. Competencies required to become a voting, responsible citizen and a holder of an occupation in the modern, complex society take a longer time to acquire, particularly since they often cannot be acquired in a 'natural' or functional setting. Given the

disjunction between child rearing and production, only a limited part of this preparation can take place under parental auspices. The family mainly serves as an agent of emotional support and reproduction.

(4) Existing institutions have increasingly taken over child care and child rearing and emerging new *ad hoc* institutions have proliferated. The regular common school has been prolonged with additional mandatory years of attendance. Day care centres and kindergartens have sprung up, particularly as the number of working mothers has increased, in many countries without being able, however, to meet the demand. Youth centres have been set up with the task of taking care of children after school hours before the parents return from their work and of youngsters who have finished school and begun to work (of whom many, however, are unemployed).

A new, in recent decades rapidly growing, class of public employees, teachers, social workers and welfare administrators, has emerged and constitutes a powerful group which knows how to take care of its interests. The drive for more public service is evidently also a self-serving one. The more 'clients,' the more jobs.

The services provided by the new class of social and welfare workers in education, poverty relief, pre-school education and regular school education are highly specialized and fragmented. Attempts to serve the whole child run up against what has been referred to as 'the iron web of bureaucratization' (Cerych, 1977). Youth problems, such as unemployment, drug abuse, and delinquency, are dealt with by different specialized agencies enviously protecting their own turfs. A thoroughly coordinated overall therapy administered to individuals or groups is difficult, not to say impossible, to achieve under such circumstances. Actions by public agencies are taken along 'vertical' instead of 'horizontal' lines.

The bureaucracy constitutes an 'iron web' when it comes to attempts to deal with the 'youth problem.' The public sector today has built-in rigidities that prevent the implementation of concerted policies designed to cope with various social pathologies that beset the youth, such as apathy, drug abuse, delinquency, and vandalism. It is, however, in the interest of the growing class of public functionaries to keep young people not only from the streets but from productive life as well, because this would imply a diminishing role for themselves and put their jobs in jeopardy.

The symposium cited above reached the conclusion that 'there is in contemporary industrial society a youth problem of extraordinary, unprecedented, and worsening proportions—lying beyond the reach of macroeconomic, countercyclical measures and defying established institutional approaches' (Cerych, 1977, p. 10).

There has in recent decades in all industrialized societies been a shift of responsibility from the family to the institutions. In his analysis of the 'asymmetric society' Coleman (1981) points out that the institutions involved in child rearing in today's society are not extensions of the traditional family, 'the last kernel of the old social structure to remain.' The family is, in a way, a 'legal anachronism' which is difficult to sustain in a society consisting of growing, powerful organizations where 'persons are transient and only the structure is permanent' (p. 122). There is a sharp discontinuity between the dominant social structure consisting of institutions on the one hand and the family on the other. The new structure is built upon *activities* and not on persons. The membership in a family is what sociologists use to refer to as 'ascribed,' whereas membership in the organizations referred to as modern 'corporate actors' is 'achieved,' an outcome of initiative on the part of the individual or the 'corporate actor.'

The incompatibilities between the responsibility of the parents and the society represented by growingly powerful institutions, each with its responsibilities for one aspect or segment of the child, have brought about problems of crisis format, particularly among children who are growing up in disadvantaged and deprived milieux. The 'ecology' of upbringing has become increasingly fragmented and impersonal, particularly for children growing up in large cities with large schools. For instance, it was recently found that in five large cities in the United States 84 per cent of the high school students were attending schools with an enrollment above 2,000 students (Timpane *et al.*, 1976). Secondary schools have by the consolidation process become pedagogical superfactories.

Young Adulthood as a 'New' Stage of Life

As we have seen above, transition to adulthood has traditionally been defined by a series of legal criteria, such as the age when a marriage licence can be obtained, when the individual is allowed to undertake certain economic transactions or has the right to vote. But in addition one has applied criteria of being able to support oneself, to be independent of one's family, etc. But all these criteria are far from perfectly correlated. In addition, they have in recent times tended to become less correlated, which reflects the blurring of the borderline between youth and adulthood. Young people can, for instance, have the right to vote in general elections but be subjected to regulations by educational institutions acting *in loco parentis*.

But there are changes of a fundamental nature in modern society that affect the status of young people to the extent that there is ample reason to talk about youth as a 'new stage in life.' Our attention to this was drawn by the 'youth revolt' in the late 1960s and early 1970s. Keniston (1970) in an article in *The American Scholar* advanced the notion that societal changes had brought about a 'new' stage of life following after what traditionally had been conceived as adolescence. He pointed out that several factors, such as rising prosperity, prolongation of formal education, increased educational demands by a post-industrial society that had contributed to creating an 'adolescent society,' also were behind an emerging youth phase *following* adolescence.

Rapid social changes have affected old institutions and values. The impact of the new technology that threatens to destroy the world, the instant communication that made young people aware of the wars, the suffering and injustices around the globe, all have contributed to inspiring concerns among young people in the age range between 18 and 24. At first there were 'forerunners' of youngsters of university age with a heightened awareness of the vicissitudes of a world under the impact of the Vietnam War. Since then, a growing number of post-adolescents are characterized by the fact that 'they have not settled the questions whose answers once defined adulthood: questions of relationships to the existing society, questions of vocation, questions of social role and life-style' (Keniston, 1970, p. 634). Keniston's thesis is that 'we are witnessing today the emergency on a mass scale of a previously unrecognized stage of life,' a stage between adolescence and adulthood (*op. cit.*, p. 635). He tries to define youth by defining the major themes that dominate young people's consciousness, behaviour and development during this age and the specific changes in various domains (moral, intellectual, sexual, etc.) of development that occur during this stage. There is a consensus among those who have studied adolescence that the lower limit of the period is defined by physiological criteria, puberty and a growth spurt in height and weight. There also seems to be a consensus about criteria for setting the upper limit of youth. They are all *social* criteria, for instance taking on certain adult responsibilities, ability to support oneself by work, readiness to vote and for marriage, etc. The problem, however, is that these criteria are rather spread out in time. Young people are 'adults' in certain respects, for instance with regard to voting age, but dependent youngsters in other respects, for instance with regard to authority to conduct their own business.

There is furthermore general agreement that adolescence and youth is a period when young people try to explore themselves and the future roles they envisage. They are not only exploring but also trying out various options. It is a stage which Erik Erikson (1968) refers to as a 'psychological moratorium,' a period which in modern, complex society has become increasingly difficult, because more options and alternatives (educational, vocational and marital) are open than in a more static society. Young people need access to meaningful alternatives without premature commitments. This means by necessity that the age when they more definitely assume adult roles has tended to move up.

Clark Kerr (1977) has proposed a two-stage conception of youth which, in a way, is an extension of the scheme proposed by Charlotte Bühler

(1921) in her study of the psychology of the adolescent in the early 1920s. After the advent of puberty comes a period of psychological maturation, exploration and 'floundering.' Given the fact that a growing proportion of young people are in institutions of education until their early twenties, it is convenient to distinguish between adolescence and youth.

Changing Values and Attitudes

Controversy about the 'real nature' of youth and what is at the core of the 'youth problem' often stems from a confusion of two main phenomena associated with youth: the 'generation gap' in terms of values and attitudes and the institutional segregation of young people from adult society. Both phenomena are regarded either as symptoms or as conditions conducive to disjunction, counterculture and revolt. But there is little evidence in support of the notion of a *general* gap in value-orientation between young people and their elders. Even during the upheaval and revolt in the late 1960s, a movement in most countries spearheaded by university-based, upper-middle class youngsters, surveys showed a remarkable unanimity in value-orientation even between the so-called militants and their parents.

The universalization of secondary education and mass higher education has led to a prolonged period of institutional segregation for the majority of young people from fifteen to the early twenties. Whether the fact that young people spend most of their time in school instead of at work places justifies talking about segregation has been widely discussed in the wake of the Coleman (1974) report on youth. Both the concept of a 'generation gap' and that of segregation have been challenged. Some participants in the debate on youth problems have even raised the question whether there is any special youth problem at all.

Youth can be conceived as a period of both reproduction and transformation. Young people become socialized by their family, school, and peers. They internalize prevailing values of these agents. The preponderance of one of them over the others varies beteen generations and social groups. But socialization is not 'perfect' in the sense that the youngsters indiscriminately accept values of the older generation or of their peers. There is always a margin of freedom in the *selection* of values which guide the socialization process. This is noticeable among the more articulate young people leading the youth movement. They are 'forerunners' who herald new paradigms of thought and new valuations. The new values then spread to the big masses of youngsters.

A general change in values in the affluent society has occurred over the last few decades among young people. Somewhat schematically it can be said that *expressive* values have gained in importance relative to *instrumental* ones. A change towards expressive values can be traced behind the quest for improved quality of life and the increased emphasis on spiritual and humanistic pursuits in opposition to the pragmatic and technological ones.

In assessing the changing values Yankelovich (1972) made a distinction between two categories of young: 'forerunners' and the 'practically-minded.' The forerunners according to Havighurst's (1975) estimate make up some 20 per cent of the age group 15 to 25. They more frequently dissent from their parents about social and political issues; they want social changes that play down the consumer society and emphasize values of self-expression and arts. The 'dissenters' and 'young radicals' constitute a sub-group among the forerunners. They are oriented towards expressive values and want to use their education to criticize society rather than as a means of perpetuating a growth-oriented, technological society. The practically-oriented, on the one hand, are, as Havighurst (1975) put it, 'the apprentices to the leaders of the technocratic, production oriented, instrumental society.' They endorse values of productivity, achievement motivation, materialism, and social responsibility ('law and order'). They comprise in his estimation some 60 per cent of the youth of 15 to 25. The remaining 20 per cent consists of 'left-outs' who are the less educated, less articulate, and, in my terminology, recruits of the 'new underclass.'

Changing Attitudes to Education and Work

The rapidly increasing availability of further-going education (beyond the mandatory) has led to a revolution of rising expectations. These include hopes about the status and the nature of the jobs which additional schooling and the ensuing credentials will entitle those who 'stick it out.'

Young people and their parents are keenly aware of the decisive role played by formal education in determining future social role and job status. Therefore, even those who heed quite negative attitudes to the content of education offered by the institutions they attend, are ready to embark on long courses of study in order to push themselves as far up as possible on the ladder of general education. They realize perfectly well that the amount of formal education they have absorbed will decide the place they will occupy not only in the line seeking entry to the next level of education but in the line of job seekers as well. They are also aware of the fact that, in spite of much talk about 'over-education' and unemployment among university graduates, holders of basic degrees are several times less likely to become unemployed after leaving school than are secondary school leavers, not to mention drop-outs.

In the six-subject survey conducted by the International Association for the Evaluation of Educational Achievement (IEA) student attitudes towards schooling in general as well as towards the importance of success in school were assessed. Students in industrialized and affluent countries, such as Sweden and the Federal Republic of Germany, tended to score low on the attitude scale, whereas students in developing countries with miserable school facilities scored very high. One reasonable explanation—lacking further evidence—is that there are so many other agents in affluent countries which compete with the school, such as media, sports and other leisure time activities. But since the negativism among students from affluent countries tends to increase during the last stage of mandatory school, another reasonable explanation is the growing awareness among young people of circumstances, not least rising youth unemployment, that frustrate their hopes and aspirations. Young people are aware of the increased competition in school and the world of work and of the role played by the school as a sorting and sifting device. They are also aware of the importance of marks and examinations as part of the selection game they have to go through in order to reach as far up as possible on the ladder of formal schooling.

In spite of all the rhetoric to the contrary, credentialism tends to gain ground (Teichler, 1976; Dore, 1976). The classic, ideal picture of young people, who after careful guidance and realizing their 'real abilities and bents' successively approach the occupational domain and the particular job of their personal choice, contrasts with the grim reality facing many youngsters, namely that of negative choice made for them at an early stage by the school.

The intense, not to say aggressive, debate in recent years in many countries about school marks, examinations and *numerus clausus* reflects a reaction against credentialism among the more articulate (and vociferous) students. No doubt the emotional heat of the debate about school marks in countries which have gone through the enrollment explosion stage is fuelled by the fact that school marks are instruments of competition. A vociferous minority of students is fighting against them because of a change in values that has had repercussions on a broad range of issues in the political domain. Marks are conceived as instruments of the capitalist, free market system society, with an educational system educating young people for the 'slots' in the employment system, without consideration of intrinsic, educational values. The sorting and sifting performed by the school is seen as subservience to the forces on the labor market. It is also pointed out that the marking and ranking of individual performances are not compatible with the values expressed in curricular rhetoric on education for co-operation, self-fulfillment and personal initiative.

However, the opinion among students on the marking and ranking system is highly divided. Opinion polls show that the majority of students would prefer marks to other types of individual assessment. This majority tends to be more silent than the active minority. One could venture the diagnosis that quite a lot of pragmatism goes into the attitude of the less vociferous majority. The reality of meritocracy is there. The school cannot do away with it simply because it is not operating in a social vacuum. In my book *Talent, Equality and Meritocracy* (Husén, 1974) I have raised the question if and to what extent a certain meritocratic element is an intrinsic element of the high technology society and whether the drawbacks of meritocracy constitute the prize paid for keeping the machinery running and the economy growing.

Lack of systematic evidence, particularly comparative evidence, covering a long period, makes it hard to judge to what extent changes in attitudes towards education and work have taken place among different categories of young people. Student activism referred to above on questions of marks, examinations and participation in decision-making is a symptom of such a change. Confrontations between students and decision-making bureaucracies are other symptoms. On the side of occasional and local eruptions one can trace what fittingly could be called a 'quiet revolution' inspired by values and attitudes guiding redefinitions of work, success and quality of life.

It should again be underscored that the 'new values' are more pronounced among the better educated and articulated young people but are in the process of spreading to the entire youth generation.

Salient features of this change are:

(1) The notion of a successful career as a continuous advantage and promotion in a process of selection and competition, where the able and ambitious succeed and the others fail, is rejected. More emphasis is placed on self-fulfillment, security, and development of rewarding leisure time interests. Intrinsic satisfaction tends to be preferred to instrumental satisfaction in both education and work. One typical objection against relative school marks, which rank students, is that they make students work for marks and not for the rewards ensuing from the acquisition of useful and developing competencies.

(2) Education should try to attain the wider range of objectives espoused in the rhetoric of education bills, curricular preambles, and commencement speeches. Studies are not for narrow vocational goals only but for the development of the whole personality. The over-arching purpose of education at any stage is to prepare the individual to become a creative and participating citizen. Reforms of, for instance, higher education advanced under the auspices of enrollment explosion, limited resources and 'management of decline' have aimed at university programmes narrowly defined in terms of vocational competencies. Such reforms or reform proposals in, for instance, Sweden and France have been strongly rejected by the students who resent being prepared for vocational 'slots.' They do not resent study programmes linked to action—the enthusiasm with which cross-disciplinary programmes focussing on major social problems has been met bears witness to this. But they want a

more proper balance between humanistic education and practical preparation. Above all, the resentment is strong against programmes which lead to specific occupational competencies, because of the feeling of being locked into a particular occupation with limited leeway for a career change. They want education to prepare them for a broad range of—largely unforeseen—tasks that they might encounter in a dynamic society where the individual wants to have more degrees of freedom for his career decisions.

(3) There is a growing realization among young people who are actively reacting against competition and credentialism to conceive education as something that in the future in different ways can be 'mixed' into the career pattern. The growing number of students who do not any longer take their entire formal education *en bloc*, but 'step out' for a certain period before proceeding with, for instance, university studies, is an important symptom of changed attitudes.

(4) Concomitant with the rapidly rising level of formal education among entrants to the world of work, and to a large extent an outcome of it, is the profound change occurring in the perception of what work means. I have already pointed out the trend towards emphasis on intrinsic or expressive instead of instrumental or extrinsic satisfaction.

(5) The quest for self-fulfillment and meaningfulness applies to work as well as to education. This is part of what above was referred to as the 'revolution of rising expectations.' Young people increasingly want to hold jobs which allow them a certain margin of freedom in terms of personal initiative. They want to have more say about the working conditions and the planning of the work process. They do not accept the drudgery and boredom which their elders had to put up with.

(6) There is today a marked tendency among young people in highly industrialized and affluent societies to push upward the age when they feel it appropriate to 'settle down.' A leading expert of vocational guidance, Donald Super, talks about a stage of 'floundering' in the development of vocational maturity.

In 1975 an international colloquium *Adolescence in the Year 2000* was organized in Amsterdam by the *Jeugdprofiel 2000* with participation of scholars representing relevant social science disciplines and areas of experience. The report (Hill and Mönks, 1977) points out that: 'Adolescence as we know it in modern societies is a creature of the industrial revolution and it continues to be shaped by forces which defined that revolution: industrialization, specialization, urbanization, the rationalization and bureaucratization of human organizations and institutions, and continuing technological development.' The result of this has been that the period of transition between childhood and adulthood has become extended, a development that has been further reinforced by the earlier onset of physical puberty and the universalization of secondary education. This also means increased segregation of adolescents. 'The next 25 years will see the continuation of these trends, one important example being an increase in the proportion of young people who go on for post-secondary education and training, thus further postponing the assumption of fully adult responsibilities . . . The continued bureaucratization of institutions in society, the lack of attractiveness of existing youth organizations, a continued growth in size of organizations which serve adolescents and their families, and the trend towards centralized social planning at local and national levels seem likely to bring a greater homogenization of norms, ideologies, behaviours and experience' (*op. cit.*, pp. 244–245). There are also other forces that work towards uniformity in norms and other frames of reference, for instance the development of global communication and the quest for equality within and across nations.

The pervasive problem of adolescence in all times and all societies has been the development of *identity*, which can easily become more acute in the mass media society with its pressure for uniformity. The right to differ, the recognition of diversity in the adolescent experience, the pluralism of values in society, the right to make choices and the right to explore more thoroughly the options in terms of adult roles could become overriding issues in the future.

References

Andersson, B-E. (1969) *Studies in Adolescent Behaviour* (Stockholm, Almqvist and Wiksell).
Andersson, B-E. (1982) *Generation efter generation* (Generation after Generation) (Malmö, Liber).
Andersson, B-E. and Wallin, E. (1971) *Tonåringarna och omvärlden* (Teenagers and Their World) (Stockholm, Almqvist and Wiksell).
Boocock, S. (1973) *An Introduction to the Sociology of Learning* (Boston, Houghton Mifflin).
Bühler, C. (1921) *Das Seelenleben des Jugendlichen* (Jena, Fischer).
Cerych, L. (Ed.) (1977) *Youth—Education—Employment*, Proceedings of an International Symposium held at Fère-en-Tardenois, France, 27–30 April (Amsterdam, European Cultural Foundation).
Coleman, J. S. (1961) *The Adolescent Society: The social life of the teenager and its impact on education* (Glencoe, Free Press).
Coleman, J. S. (1981) *The Asymmetric Society* (Syracuse, Syracuse University Press).
Coleman, J. S. and Husén, T. (1985) *Becoming Adult in a Changing Society* (Paris, OECD).
Dore, R. (1976) *The Diploma Disease: Education, Qualification and Development* (London, Allen and Unwin).
Erikson, E. (1968) *Identity, Youth and Crisis* (New York, Norton).
Eisenstadt, S. N. (1957) *From Generation to Generation* (Glencoe, Free Press).
Hall, G. S. (1904) *Adolescence and Its Relations to Psychology, Anthropology, Sociology, Sex, Crime, Religion and Education*, I–II (New York, Appleton).
Hall, G. S. (1923) *Life and Confessions of a Psychologist* (New York, Appleton).
Havighurst, R. J. and Drever, Ph. H. (1975) *Youth: The Seventyfourth Yearbook of the National Society for the Study of Education* (Chicago, The University of Chicago Press).
Hill, J. P. and Mönks, F. J. (Eds) (1977) *Adolescence and Youth in Prospect*, Proceedings of an international colloquium *Jeugdprofiel 2000* held in Amsterdam 17–18 September 1975 (Guildford, Surrey, PCS Science and Technology Press).
Hollingshead, A. B. (1949) *Elmstown Youth* (New York, Wiley).

Husén, T. (1944) *Adolescensen, Undersökningar rörande manlig svensk ungdom i åldern 17–20 år* (Adolescence. Investigations of Male Swedish Youth of the Ages 17–20) (Uppsala, Almqvist and Wiksell).

Husén, T. (1974) *Talent, Equality and Meritocracy* (The Hague, Nijhoff).

Husén, T. (1979) *The School in Question: A Comparative Study of the School and Its Future in Western Societies* (London, Oxford University Press).

Keniston, K. (1968) *Young Radicals* (New York, Harcourt, Brace and World).

Keniston, K. (1968) Youth, change and violence, *The American Scholar*, 37(2) pp. 227–245.

Keniston, K. (1970) Youth: a new stage of life, *The American Scholar*, 39(4) pp. 631–654.

Keniston, K. (1971) *Youth and Dissent* (New York, Harcourt, Brace and Jovanovich).

Kerr, C. (1977) Education and the world of work: an analytical sketch, in: Perkins, J. A. and Burn, B. (Eds) *International Perspective on Problems in Higher Education*, pp. 132–142 (New York, International Council for Educational Development).

Kerr, D. (1983) Teaching competence and teacher education in the United States, *Teachers College Record*, 84(3) pp. 525–552.

Mead, M. (1928) *Coming of Age in Samoa: A psychological study of primitive youth for Western civilisation* (New York, William Morrow).

Passow, A. H. (1975) Once again: Reforming secondary education, *Teachers College Record*, 77(2) pp. 161–187.

Silberman, C. E. (1970) *Crisis in the Classroom: The remaking of American education* (New York, Random House).

Spranger, E. (1924) *Psychologie des Jugendalters* (Leipzig, Quelle and Meyer).

Tanner, J. M. (1962) *Growth at Adolescence*, 2nd ed. (Oxford, Blackwell Scientific).

Teichler, U. (1976) *Das Dilemma der modernen Bildungsgesellschaft* (Stuttgart, Klett).

Timpane, M. *et al.* (1976) *Youth Policy in Transition* (Santa Monica, California, Rand).

Yankelovich, D. (1972) *Changing Values on Campus: political and personal attitudes on campus* (New York, Washington Square Press).

4

Integration of General and Vocational Education: An International Perspective

EDUCATION IS an enterprise with a distant time perspective. The young people we have in school today are going to have their most productive years decades from now, well into the twenty-first century in a society and in an economy that in important respects will look rather different. Thus in reflecting on vocational education serving those who are going to work in the next century it would be in order to adopt a futuristic perspective.

In the late 1960s futurological investigations became fashionable among planners and policymakers. They began to realize that plans drawn up and decisions taken today have fundamental implications for the social system of tomorrow, implications that, due to the rapidity of change in modern society and the emergence of unforeseen circumstances, are worthy of consideration. Futurological studies are therefore regarded as instruments not in the first place to predict but to spell out probable alternative consequences of decisions and/or actions taken today. Thus those who devote themselves to futurological exercises are trying to work out *possible* scenarios. In writing future scenarios for education one has to start with a set of assumptions about the societal conditions under which education in the future most likely will have to operate. Even with the strong qualification that such scenarios are not telling what *will* happen but *could* happen, given the decisions we take today, the exercise of envisaging the future is, indeed, a very hazardous one. In spite of being 'right' about major conditions in the future, wrong assumptions about one or two of them can lead planners and policymakers astray.

In my capacity as a social scientist I was in the years 1968–70 involved in a major futurological study supported by the Swedish National Board of Education (Husén, 1971). The time perspective for the study was the one that futurologists at that time tended to draw up, namely the year 2000.

More than a decade later UNESCO invited me to write a paper on present trends and tendencies in education with a perspective on the future. The paper was part of a future-oriented project the agency was then conducting (Husén, 1982). Since this was a point in time almost halfway between the late 1960s and the turn of the century I could in preparing the paper not refrain from checking the conditions I had assumed in the late 1960s. In my paper I pointed out that with regard to educational planning there were two highly relevant changes with impact on education that had not been foreseen in the previous study. In the first place, the dramatic downturn of the birthrate, although it had already started in the 1960s in Western industrial countries, had been over-looked. As late as in 1964 Georg Picht had published his alarming book *Die deutsche Bildungskatastrophe* and had pointed out that the big dis-crepancy in size between older and younger age groups in Germany would result in an extremely serious shortage of teachers. Even if all young people who took *Abitur* (secondary school certificate) became teachers they would not cover the demand. Soon the birthrate went down to half of what it had been before. Second, the 'stagflation' in the wake of the oil crisis brought about a situation of austerity which in many countries had a strong impact on the financial situation of the school systems. In the 1960s unbroken economic growth was predicted.

Evidently both these new conditions had profound consequences for educational policy and planning. Education tended in the industrial countries to slip down on the political priority scale. The number of those with a stake in education diminished. By the early 1960s in some countries about 40 per cent of the voters had own children in school or at the universities. By the mid-1980s the proportion had decreased to about 20 per cent.

The Working Life Setting

The forces which will have an impact on the labor market today and tomorrow can be categorized under three main headings: (1) High tech-nology, such as computerization, biotechnology and new communication systems; (2) market competition, internationally and regionally within nations; and (3) new forms of work organization, particularly parti-cipatory ones. All three have implications for the educational system, including vocational education and the training for specific occupations.

Will the new technology, which recently has invaded our daily life, have a decisive impact on the employment structure? The answer is, surprisingly enough, close to an unqualified no. Predictions made by means of sophisticated techniques tend to show that *relatively* few new job opportunities will be generated until the end of the century by high technology. For instance, the Bureau of Labor Statistics in the United

States has estimated that advanced technology will generate only 6 per cent of the new jobs, whereas 70 per cent will be generated in the service sector, such as health care, retail business, and public administration.

Even though the new types of jobs generated in the hi-tech sectors are going to increase employment considerably in a *relative* sense, they will *absolutely* constitute a small increase in employment opportunities in comparison with all the manifold service jobs in supermarkets, restaurants, hospitals, day care centers, old age institutions, etc.

What do the changes occurring in working life imply in terms of qualification requirements for the labor force? The machines have long ago taken over most of the physical labor. At the turn of the century at least one third of the work force consisted of pure manual labor. Now it is down to only 5–6 per cent.

In the 1950s a wave of new technology introduced under the label 'automation' led to fears about mass unemployment. But the expanding economy supporting an expanding public service sector succeeded to absorb those who lost their jobs due to the rationalization of production in the manufacturing industry.

The outcomes of the new high technology wave which is in the process of affecting the industrial societies has, as we now see, led to high unemployment among those with poor formal and vocational schooling. This applies in particular to countries which do not have a policy of full employment by means of public works and labor-market training and retraining.

Will 'over-education' occur as a result of the enormous expansion of the formal system of schooling? I do not think so. Citizens in a complex society with participatory democracy need to be equipped with a broad and solidly based repertoire of competencies, skills and knowledge, in order to master their own destiny. Advanced formal education along with special vocational qualifications is the best insurance a person in our society can have against unemployment. It will also serve as a good basis for further general education and special vocational training.

Implications of High Technology for the System of Education

Attempts to predict what will happen in the educational system as a result of ongoing technological changes depend very much on how the third force pointed out above, the work organization, will develop in the future. The classical industrial model of this organization has been a hierarchical one, where the worker is performing a limited set of work operations under strict control and with little scope for his or her own initiative. One has begun to realize that this model does not work in present-day society with an increasingly well-educated work force.

Experiences gained, for instance in car manufacturing at the Volvo company in Sweden, have shown that workers' participation in a flexible work process can be a decisive factor in enhancing production and efficiency.

If a development along participatory lines takes place in the future, changes in curricula designed to provide future-oriented vocational education are called for. The traditional objective of providing skills and knowledge of a rather limited and specific nature would have to yield to competencies which cover a broader range of situations—both within and outside the work place. The central capacity that an individual in modern society needs to possess is the ability to learn—and re-learn. The ability to acquire knowledge on one's own is essential in a society where the majority of employees are forced to take further courses in order to keep up and to enhance their qualifications. In fact, most workers today will face a situation where they have to change their occupation at least once during their career.

In the service and information sectors the ability to read and write, and to communicate with one's fellows, is of crucial importance in succeeding as a citizen in general and an employee in particular. It is therefore distressing that many young people nowadays leave school after nine to ten years with poor communication skills which make them unemployable in a labor market where these skills have become essential.

In addition, everybody in the present and the future society needs to become 'literate' in science. I am referring not only to a basic knowledge of physics, chemistry, biology, and the earth sciences. What has become increasingly important in an industrial world beset with ecological problems is the ability to use this knowledge to judge the impact of science and technology on our daily life, both now and in the future. People have begun to talk about 'new science' as a school subject, relevant to a society in which technology is threatening to put the environment in jeopardy.

It is, indeed, essential in a complex society and an equally demanding working life that school education fosters critical thinking and trains the ability to tackle problems both co-operatively and independently. Such competencies are of crucial importance if employees are required increasingly to participate in the production process and to take the initiative to solve problems.

The school in highly industrial societies is often—when it comes to training young people to handle human relations and not least those in the work place—faced with a contradiction between rhetoric and reality. I have dealt with this and other contradictions in my book *The School in Question* (Husén, 1979). The curricular rhetoric talks about education for co-operation, loyalty and responsibility *vis-à-vis* other people, not least those in the work place. But the reality is that modern, industrial society has become increasingly competitive and meritocratic. Social status is, to a large extent, determined by school attainments. It is the individual achievement that counts. Formal education has increasingly become the first criterion of selection among job seekers. Those who fail in school are at best assigned to the least attractive jobs and at worst become unemployed (Coleman and Husén, 1985).

A UNESCO Experience

Many years ago, in the late 1950s, UNESCO invited a group of education experts to a committee charged with the task of preparing more or less universal curricular guidelines for secondary education. I happened to serve as chairman at a session in Paris when the relationship between general and vocational education was the major item on our agenda. We spent two full days trying to arrive at a consensus about what should be meant by 'general' education. Our French colleague with experience as *Inspecteur Générale de l'Instruction Publique* advanced the view that general education was the goal of the *culture générale* that was embodied in the curriculum of the French *lycée*. The Soviet colleague, one of the Vice-Presidents of the Academy of Pedagogical Sciences, proposed that Soviet polytechnical education was in essence general education. Our American colleague, superintendent of a big city school system, defined general education as the competencies all citizens needed in order to get along in life, including driver education!

It was not easy to bring these different conceptions to a common denominator. The main reason for our difficulties was, of course, that even if there are certain general philosophical considerations and principles, which pervade different cultures and national boundaries, the concrete and operational manifestations of these considerations vary from one nation or a culture to the other. What the school needs to equip a young person growing up in a highly industrial and technological society differs quite a lot from the subsistence competencies to which the school contributes in a developing society. Length, structure, and content of schooling by necessity vary with social and economic conditions.

The issue of general versus vocational education has an epistemological dimension with close bearings on the 'utility' of educational research, a problem that I have recently dealt with in an article for the UNESCO journal *Prospects* (Husén, 1989). The crucial problem I am highlighting is that research cannot straightforwardly 'tell' the classroom practitioner what to do in a particular situation. There exists no clearcut linear relationship of applicability between the generalizations offered by psychology, sociology, or the other social sciences and the actual school situation with a class and a child here and now. At best such research can offer a perspective and a framework for the use of a common sense and experience derived from previous work and practice in the classroom. My Stanford colleague Elliot Eisner talks about 'connoisseurship' as the essence of teacher competence. It consists of the competence that must lie behind the understanding of the particular classroom situation and the particular child. This also applies to vocational education: the 'practical' has to fill the abstract and theoretical with sensible content.

A Comparative Perspective

In looking at the secondary, particularly upper-secondary, school provisions in terms of structure and curricula in a cross-national, comparative perspective, we can identify three models.

(1) The *bi-partite*, traditional European model where academic and vocational schools coexist as parallels. Their enrollments differ considerably with regard to student social background. The two types of schools show a high disparity of esteem and a low degree of mobility between themselves.

(2) The *comprehensive* model with highly diversified curricular provisions and with all the programs under the same roof. The American comprehensive high school is the classical model. Recently, the Swedish 'gymnasium school' has become another example.

(3) The *dual* model which is the prevailing one in the Federal Republic of Germany with a university-preparing, academic Gymnasium for the elite and the apprenticeship system for the remainder with part-time formal instruction and practice in the enterprises.

Interestingly, the last couple of decades have shown an increasing convergence between the three models, at least in the industrialized countries. In the United States of America, not least initiated by the National Commission for Excellence at the Federal level and subsequently by a lot of state and local commissions, there has been a strong pressure for strengthening the academic curriculum. In the East European countries there has been a growing realization that students pursuing vocational programs ought to be provided with an upgraded general education. In Sweden it has been found that those in the vocational tracks need to get a better and extended instruction in the mother tongue and in other general subjects.

There is also a tendency across models and countries to break up the traditional institutionalization in secondary formal school locations and increasingly to move to new settings provided by either industry and business or by community institutions, such as youth service centers and youth co-operatives.

The Swedish Experience

The changing conception over the last few decades of the role of vocational education in the system of public schooling can be illustrated by the

Swedish school reforms. I am not citing Sweden as an example for other countries but simply as an illustration of a reform development that has taken place under great political stability and—by and large—under political consensus. It also illustrates the process of convergence mentioned above.

The first phase of the reform, taking place from the mid-1940s up to the Education Act establishing a basic nine-year school in 1962, aimed at abolishing the 'parallel system,' where a social and intellectual elite could transfer to the academic secondary school after four years of elementary school whereas the remainder stayed on until compulsory attendance expired after six or seven years. All school types covering the first nine years of schooling were integrated into a common, 9-year, 'basic' school. The main issue was to what extent there should be a 'differentiation' of programs during the upper stage, i.e., grades 7 through 9. The pilot program of comprehensive education during the 1950s had three tracks, one academic (with two foreign languages), one vocational and one 'general,' a system similar to the one of the British Education Act of 1944. During the ninth school year, the 'theoretically oriented' took a 'pre-gymnasium' program and the 'practically oriented' had some pre-vocational training. They were taught in separate classes.

In the years preceding the 1962 Act there had been a heated debate on what was referred to as 'differentiation' both organizationally and pedagogically (Husén, 1962). In a book published in 1961 under the title *The School in a Changing Society* I took the standpoint that one should try to postpone organizational differentiation as far up in the system as possible and try to keep all students in a common core program. This would provide the competencies needed for all citizens in a democratic and technologically changing society and provide them with a common frame of reference of knowledge and basic values. The longer the differentiation between the 'theoretical' and 'practical' was delayed the less would be the influence of social background on educational opportunity and career.

The idea at the beginning of the reform period of introducing at an early age elements of 'pure' vocational training derived from the concept of a static society. The specific vocational competencies acquired today were seen as equally useful tomorrow. But in a rapidly changing job structure it is hard to predict what qualifications will be useful even a few years hence and in order to play it safe one should prepare the young people for a society and a working life in flux, giving them a solid basis of skills and basic concepts in science and technology which can be applied to a broad spectrum of situations and tasks, many of which are unforeseen.

The consequence of such a concept of basic education ought to be a common, general curriculum with a core of communication skills, scientific literacy and a frame of reference of historical and civic orientation.

The 1962 Act which made provisions for the new nine-year basic school implied three streams at the upper section, where from grade 7 certain elective subjects could be taken which lead up to three separate sections in grade 9, from which transfer could take place to academic or vocational schools at the upper secondary stage (grades 10 through 12). According to a prediction based on the pilot program, roughly one third of the students in grade 7 would opt for the academic track. Very soon it turned out to be about two thirds of the students. Thus, the majority did not feel attracted by the vocational program. In less than ten years, when the Minister of Education signed the objectives and guidelines for the next national curriculum in the basic school there was a core curriculum for *all* students up through grade 9. The electives did not earmark the students for any particular subsequent program. A fully integrated basic school without pre-vocational instruction had emerged.

In the late 1960s the next stage, grades 10 through 12, which in Swedish terminology were referred to as the 'gymnasium school,' was completely restructured with the aim of catering to the great majority. It changed from being a university-preparing elite school serving less than 10 per cent of the age group to a continuation school for some 90 per cent of young people. It offered more than twenty programs, most of them vocationally-oriented two-year courses whereas the academic programs covered three years. About one third of those who continued upper secondary education entered the three-year academic programs. The interesting experience is that it has been possible to attract highly able students with good marks in grade 9 to the vocational programs. One motivating factor to enter such programs has been that all students with a two-year program and with a certain minimum mark in mother tongue and English possess general entrance qualification for higher education. This has, of course, contributed to enhance the prestige and attractiveness of the vocational programs.

The experiences gained during the almost two decades which have elapsed since the upper secondary school reform have shown two weaknesses. One drawback has been the time available. 'General' subjects, particularly the mother tongue, had to yield to instruction in the directly vocationally useful parts of the curriculum. Teachers and the enterprises which employed the young people were complaining about deficient basic skills, particularly in writing and in reading comprehension. Thus, recently the Swedish *Riksdag* passed a bill according to which a three-year vocational program on a pilot basis is introduced in a large number of gymnasium schools. The extension of the vocational programs is, of course, another factor that contributes to the parity of esteem with the academic programs.

Needless to say, mass secondary education, where vocational programs qualify for university entrance, is beset with problems, which, however, may have to be taken as part of the bargain if one wants to achieve the parity referred to above.

Concluding Observations

Given the changes in working life and in society at large, is formal schooling and vocational training going to be only reactive, i.e., to simply adapt to new requirements of society? Or proactive, i.e., to contribute towards making young people ready to meet the future and thereby serving as active agent of change in the context of a changing society? These questions are, indeed, fundamental for educators of today. Reformers have for a long time believed that the educational system has an important role to play in shaping a new and better society, an optimism which prevailed among American progressive educators after the First World War.

I once formulated the issue of general versus vocational education in the following paradoxical way: the best vocational education in today's rapidly changing society is a solid general education both in terms of breadth and quality. This by no means implies a down-grading of vocational education *per se*. On the contrary, it implies an upgrading of its quality, scope and, not least, prestige. Until recently the prevailing philosophical view in the Western world has been that there is a—rather limited—pool of academically talented or 'theoretically-oriented' young people who as early as possible during their school career ought to be channelled into the gymnasium (grammar school, lycée) type of schools which should take care of their preparation for the university and the professions. The 'vocationally-oriented' should be encouraged to enter 'practical' programs as early as possible in their school career in order to prepare themselves for the jobs they are heading for. They need only a modest repertoire of 'theoretical' skills and knowledge.

We have begun to enter what properly could be labelled the learning society (Husén, 1974) where formal schooling acquired early in life is just the beginning and where the rest of life for most people will be one long continuation of school. The term 'recurrent education' was coined by the then Swedish Minister of Education, Olof Palme, when he gave a keynote address at the meeting in Paris 1969 of the OECD ministers of education. Holders of all kinds of occupations should have the opportunity to take leave of absence from their jobs now and then in order to take courses which would enhance their vocational competence. They could among other things be participants in huge adult education programs, either public (as is the case with the adult gymnasia in Sweden) or private (under the auspices of personnel training programs run by the enterprises themselves). The training provided in a system of recurrent education would aim in the first place to improve the vocational competencies.

References

Coleman, J. S. and T. Husén (1985) *Becoming Adult in A Changing Society*. Paris: OECD (also in French).

Husén, T. (1961) *The School in A Changing Society*. Stockholm: Almqvist and Wiksell.

Husén, T. (1962) *Problems of Differentiation in Swedish Compulsory Schooling*. Stockholm: Norstedt, Scandinavian University Books.

Husén, T. (1969) Lifelong Learning in the 'Educative Society'. *International Review of Applied Psychology* Vol. 17, 87–99.

Husén, T. (1971) *Education in the Year 2000*. Stockholm: Swedish National Board of Education. (Also in Swedish, Russian, Polish, Arabic and Hindi).

Husén, T. (1974) *The Learning Society*. London: Methuen.

Husén, T. (1979) *The School in Question*. London: Oxford University Press.

Husén, T. (1982) Present Trends in Education. *Prospects*, Vol. 12:1, 45–46.

Husén, T. (1989) Educational Research at the Crossroads? *Prospects*, No. 3. UNESCO, Paris.

5

Observations on a Future-Oriented Education

Introduction

IN THE LATE 1960s futurological investigations, inspired not least by Herman Kahn *et al.* (1967) and Daniel Bell (1967), became fashionable among educational policy makers and planners. One had begun to realize that in a rapidly changing society plans drawn up or decisions taken today have serious implications for the social system tomorrow, implications that due to the rapidity of change or the emergence of unforeseen circumstances are worthy of consideration before they materialize. Therefore, futurological studies were regarded as instruments in the first place not to predict but to consider possible or likely consequences of decisions or actions taken today. Rightly so the purpose of the futurological exercises were not to predict what would happen, given the same trends and tendencies as those operating today, but what *could* happen should the auspices and circumstances of today change and new—and unforeseen— conditions emerge. Thus, the professionals in the field of futurological studies were eager to point out that their task was to work out *possible* 'scenarios.'

In my capacity as a social scientist I was myself involved in a major futurological study supported by the Bureau of Research and Development of the Swedish National Board of Education. The study was conducted in 1968–9. Leading Swedish educators and social scientists were brought together for 24-hour intensive seminars. The report was published in 1971 under the not too original title 'Education in the Year 2000' (Husén, 1971). It became translated into half a dozen languages. The time perspective was that which futurologists then drew up, i.e., to the year 2000.

A few years ago UNESCO invited me to write a paper on present trends and tendencies in education with a perspective on the future. The paper was part of a future-oriented study that the agency was conducting. Since this was a point in time half way between the late 1960s and the turn

45

of the century I could not avoid taking advantage of the opportunity to assess the validity of the 'predictions' made in the late 1960s. In my paper (Husén, 1981) I pointed out that with regard to educational planning there were two important and relevant changes with great impact on education that were not foreseen in the earlier study.

(1) The downturn of the birth rate had been neglected, although it had by the late 1960s already begun in the Western industrial world. As late as 1964 Georg Picht had published his book *Die deutsche Bildungskatastrophe* (The German Education Catastrophe) in which he pointed out that given the birth rate in Germany of the late 1950s and the discrepancy in size between earlier and later age groups it would not even suffice if all young people in Germany who took *Abitur* became teachers in order to cover the need for teachers in the German schools. Picht could, of course, not foresee that some years later the birth rate would have gone down to almost half of that around 1960.

(2) The 'stagflation' in the wake of the oil crisis in the mid-1970s tended to stifle the expansion of formal education, not least of enrollment, that had occurred in the 'golden sixties,' when education was riding on an expanding economy.

Evidently, both these new conditions had profound consequences for educational policy and planning. Education tended in the industrial countries to slip down on the political priority scale. By the early 1960s in some countries more than 40 per cent of the adult population had a child in school or university. By the mid-1980s the proportion was down to 20 per cent.

The Framework for Education in the Late 1980s

The task in the present chapter is easier than that in the book of the late 1960s. I am trying to look ahead ten years only. This can largely be done by diagnosing what is happening in education today and then extrapolating it into tomorrow. To use a metaphor: the writing on the wall is visible. It has to be interpreted properly, even though one may arrive at somewhat different interpretations depending on differences in values and ideology.

I shall point out some of the conditions for the formal system of education in today's highly industrialized societies, some of which are well beyond the threshold of the post-industrial stage. These societies have some interrelated characteristics which constitute a pervasive syndrome of the service-dominated, high-technology information society. Without putting these features in any order of importance I should like to point out the following five:

(1) Urbanization which, of course, is closely connected with the change from agriculture to manufacturing and then to service industries.

In a typical Western industrial society some 5–10 per cent of the working population is engaged in farming. Another 25–40 per cent is in manufacturing. The remainder, in several countries the majority of the workforce, is in service, such as public administration, health care, education and old-age care.

(2) The last few decades have witnessed drastic changes of the family structure and of the role of the family. The majority of women with children are now working outside the home. Co-habitation, increased divorce rate and lowering birth rate have made households with children the minority type of family, particularly in big cities.

(3) The conditions of a national economy are now to a large extent determined by its relations to an increasingly competitive world economy and world market. Third World countries have recently entered this competition, for instance in the textile industry, with serious repercussions on the employment opportunities in the traditional industrial countries, some of them on the threshold of a post-industrial service society.

(4) Formal education has, as pointed out earlier, increasingly become the main vehicle of social mobility and an individual career. The employment system increasingly tends to use formal schooling as the first criterion of selection among jobseekers. There are evident meritocratic tendencies in our societies of today (Husén, 1974).

(5) The absorbtive capacity of the labor market has changed dramatically from both a quantitative and a qualitative point of view. Automation and computerization, not to mention robotization, have in certain work fields drastically reduced the number of job openings. An extreme example is the printing industry which, as has recently been seen in the United Kingdom, has strongly affected newspaper production. A whole category of workers has become superfluous.

The situation now, in the late 1980s, is different from that in the 1960s when automation had begun to be implemented. We then had a rapidly growing economy which meant that areas in the service sector, such as health care and education, could absorb those who were made superfluous by automation and rationalization in the manufacturing industry. Now we have robotization without the leeway provided earlier by an expanding service employment. Permanent or close to permanent unemployment seems to be the fate of an increasing proportion of the work force, namely those with a minimum of formal schooling and those who are young and recently out of school. In countries without major work programs, i.e., public or subsidized jobs, the unemployment rate among the 16–19 year olds becomes very disturbing. Unemployment for these young people tends to be more or less independent of business circles which affect the employment rate among older workers.

We have begun to see a dominant feature of the meritocratic society:

unemployment, particularly among young people, is increasingly correlated with formal schooling. Recent statistics from Sweden show that unemployment among those with tertiary education is only 1 per cent, as compared to 3 per cent among those with only primary and secondary education. These figures do not include those with low formal education who are in public labor market retraining programs.

Youth has increasingly become a 'superfluous' species which is reflected in the tendency mentioned earlier that the unemployment rate among young people goes up independent of business cycles.

Consequences for School Education

Against this sketchily presented background, what are the consequences for our schools, particularly for the secondary schools, of these changes? Prolonged schooling with expanded enrollment has in recent years in many countries been the main instrument in attempts to cope with youth unemployment. But a school is a school and a workplace is a workplace. The two cannot in the long run serve as substitutes for each other.

The following deals with two overriding problems which already loom large today and are increasingly difficult for educators to come to grips with in order to make schooling, particularly at the secondary level, a meaningful experience. They are: (1) the emergence (see above) of a new educational underclass, and (2) the academization of secondary education. The tendencies implied by these two labels are closely interrelated and, I admit, constitute a major dilemma for the modern high-technology and meritocratic society.

Why do I think it appropriate to talk about a 'new' educational underclass? It differs in at least two respects from the 'old' underclass of young people who, due to their social background, were virtually excluded from advanced education during the era before the enrollment explosion. In the first place, the new underclass is a small minority and not a majority. It consists of young people from deprived—or to use a euphemism—from underprivileged homes. They are underprivileged not so much from the material as from the psychological point of view. Many are handicapped right from the first day they enter school by being psychologically undernourished, verbally understimulated and disturbed by sheer neglect. They are right from the beginning of schooling unable to live up to the expectations held by the teachers and unable to compete with their more privileged classmates. They lag behind from the outset and as they are automatically promoted from one grade to another they tend to slip behind more and more. Promotion is the easy way out: the student is just referred to the next level to another set of teachers without having to meet the minimum competence in the three Rs that was required and met by grade repeating. Thus quite a few of these youngsters complete their mandatory schooling as functional illiterates.

The 'new' underclass is, as pointed out, a minority as distinguished from the 'old' underclass which consisted of a majority or close to a majority of working class children who were excluded from high quality and furthergoing education simply for not being able to afford it in spite of being able to benefit from it. The group I am referring to as the 'new' underclass' exists in some highly industrialized countries, and particularly in their metropolitan areas, make up some 10–20 per cent of the student body. It is a small group which in contrast to the 'old' underclass has no spokesmen but to a large extent makes up the body of troublemakers in the secondary schools. Their motivation is stifled by their failures from the start, not least the failure to learn to read and write. As they enter the secondary stage of mandatory schooling they tend to perceive school as a prison and—even worse—they see no real hope in the world of work beyond school. In the permissive and euphemistic jargon of modern pedagogy they are—at least in Sweden—referred to as the 'booktired.' Many of them are gently pushed into what is by another euphemism referred to as 'adjusted courses of study.' The latter consist simply of a reduced number of hours per week in school and a certain number of working hours in an enterprise outside school, although under the supervision of guidance teachers.

But the hopelessness in school is further aggravated by the fact that what comes after completion of schooling is unemployment, at best interrupted by publicly subsidized work programs. The sombre fact in the mid-1980s was that in many OECD countries some 40–50 per cent of the 16–19 year olds out of school were unable to find work on the regular labor market (Coleman and Husén, 1985).

The young people who constitute the 'new' underclass are keenly aware of the fact that what counts on the labor market, when entry jobs are filled, is primarily the level of formal schooling attained. The jobseekers are rank-ordered according to their position on the ladder of formal education. Those who are close to the top are the first to be considered. Those on the bottom rungs are not considered at all even though they are able to cope with the few unqualified jobs available. A dilemma here, however, is that there are not many simple, traditional entry jobs any more. This is a result of the automation and rationalization that has been going on in the workplace in the last few decades. The process of rationalization is further undergirded by the trade competition both on the national and on the international market which requires increased cost-effectiveness. Enterprises simply cannot afford to pay young people the wages of fully-fledged workers for job performance that no way match these wages. The labor unions in some countries have done a disservice to the young people in this respect by trying to negotiate high wages for them.

Empirical studies of how the unemployment system recruits workers (see, for instance, Teichler, 1976) show that there is a growing tendency to use the level of formal schooling as the first criterion of selection for jobs at all levels of qualification.

The youth unemployment found in many industrial countries until the 1970s was considered to be a temporary phenomenon, such as during the Great Depression of the 1930s when unemployment struck at all age levels. What we are now experiencing is a youth unemployment that seems to be endemic and part of a larger syndrome of young people becoming superfluous outside school. Gainful employment in today's society tends not to be a characteristic of youth below the age of 20. Prolonged schooling has become the main labor market policy instrument in an era when the absorbtive capacity of the employment system has been drastically reduced due to new technology and more cost-effective use of labor. If school enrollment had not been expanded by leaps and bounds, unemployment would have been much worse, even though it is serious enough as it is.

Those who fail in school, failures that become particularly apparent at the secondary level and at the end of mandatory school attendance, leave school as illiterates who are keenly aware of their failures and in their desperation become trouble-makers. They feel that they are left-overs and can at best look forward to temporary employment in public work programs.

What has been hinted at here explains two paradoxes with which we are often confronted in secondary education in modern industrial society:

(1) Never before have so many places, in relation to the size of the age groups, been available in secondary and university education. But never before has there been such fierce competition in Europe for places at the upper secondary and tertiary levels. The system of school marks has in some countries, Sweden for one, become a major political issue. The ranking of applicants for further education has become increasingly complicated, regulated and bureaucratized.

(2) A high proportion of lower secondary school students, when their opinion is canvassed, tell us that they hate school and would leave it immediately if permitted to do so. But the majority of those who say so go on to upper secondary school 'voluntarily' after completion of mandatory school attendance. They are keenly aware of the fact that they have to 'stick it out' if they want to be considered among the ranking candidates for employment after finishing school.

We ought to step back and consider for a moment the revolutionary change that has occurred in the status of 14–18 year old people in our societies, a change that has taken place over a very short period, just a couple of decades. By the late 1940s the great majority of 14 year olds left school and entered the job market by taking typical entry jobs, such as errand boys, assisting experienced workers or simply by helping parents in small family enterprises. In countries with a tradition of apprenticeships they started as apprentices with modest wages.

By the early 1980s mandatory schooling in most industrialized countries had been extended to the age of 16, but the majority of youngsters continued their education to at least the age of 18. After completing mandatory schooling, those who try to join the work force to a large extent fail. There are simply not enough openings for young people in the world of work today. The highly rationalized, efficiency-oriented and competition-ridden working life can accommodate only full-fledged and fully productive workers.

Academization and Fragmentation of Schooling

The enrollment expansion in secondary schools, which has made school attendance at that level virtually universal, has taken place within the framework of the traditional, academically oriented type of secondary education. The school that prepared an intellectual—and social—élite for high-status, 'white-collar' jobs and for the university was the model. But the preparation for citizenship in modern society required the insertion of new subjects, such as social studies and work-studies. These were added to the traditional, academic curriculum. On top of this pre-vocational courses were introduced in certain upper secondary programs of study. The result was an overloaded secondary school curriculum. In addition to a general education program inherited from the secondary élite schools, students had to take all kinds of specialized courses given by specialized teachers.

The result of the enrollment and syllabus expansion within the traditional curriculum framework was that secondary school curricula have been suffering not only from overload but from fragmentation into many subject areas and between many teachers. It is not surprising that secondary education sometimes, not least in the American debate, has been referred to as a 'disaster area.'

What would seem to be a more obvious remedy against overload and fragmentation than to bring about differentiation between various types of students and programs and then to achieve concentration within these programs, the earlier the better? In the debate on secondary school structure that has been going on in Europe since the 1940s, it has often been taken for granted among educators that there are two main categories of students: the 'theoretically' or academically-oriented on the one hand and the 'practically' or vocationally-oriented on the other (Husén, 1986). Therefore one would have to put them into two different kinds of cur-

ricula or even different kinds of schools. Thus for the academically oriented in particular, those heading for higher education, would need a broad
base of preparatory courses in mother tongue, mathematics, science,
history and foreign languages, whereas the practically oriented would
have to take a good minimum of the 'basics', mainly the three Rs plus
general orientation courses. But the important thing for them would be to
enter pre-vocational courses as early as possible.

I shall not here enter upon any argument against such a simplistic
conception—I have discussed it at some length in many other contexts
(e.g., Husén, 1962). Nor shall I try to point out the lack of empirical
support by differential psychology (see, e.g., Härnqvist, 1961). I have for
more than thirty years almost *ad nauseam* been involved in a debate on
issues pertaining to 'differentiation.' I shall instead confine myself to
point out what I regard as the decisive argument against any organizational differentiation in mandatory schooling in a democratic society. For
such a political system to function a common frame of reference with
regard to basic cognitive competences and values is a necessary prerequisite. It is therefore essential that the school contributes to such an integration between students from different home backgrounds and walks of
life.

Life, not least the social contacts in modern society, is in so many
respects fragmented, specialized and differentiated that it is incumbent
on the school to bring about the necessary common frame of reference.
Thus, the modern complex, technological, information-flooded and com-
petence-demanding society by necessity requires a common, broad base
of general education before specific vocational competences can be
established. The dilemma that school education in our society faces is that
we cannot foresee what kinds of specific vocational competences an
individual 'needs' during his or her occupational career, not even at the
beginning. Techniques and the competence to master them come and go
and there is over the short period of a decade a radical restructuring in
many vocational fields. We know for sure that people need to be retrained
or at least take additional training within their specialist fields in order to
keep up with current changes. What is required of citizens in modern
society is enough flexibility to keep up with these changes. This requires
in its turn a solid base of skills and fundamental knowledge applicable to a
broad repertoire of unforeseen requirements and situations later in life
both inside and outside the person's occupation.

With such a perspective one can understand the paradox that the best
vocational education is a good general education.

What Changes Are Called For in the Schools?

How should we try to tackle the dual problem of the new educational underclass and the academization of secondary education? Given the necessity of keeping young people in school, not least because of the drastic reduction of employment opportunities, how do we go about making the prolonged stay in school meaningful? It is not enough to have young people institutionalized merely in order to 'keep them off the streets.' How do we make a virtue out of the necessity to extend schooling for everybody? How can we navigate between the grinding of dry, abstract knowledge on the one hand and practical trivialities on the other?

What kind of pedagogical philosophy should guide the efforts to make the universal secondary school meaningful to all its students? If we look back on pedagogical reform movements since the turn of the century, and in particular after 1918, we find many reform proposals with a common core under such labels as *Arbeitsschule* (work task school), activity pedagogy, individualization, *vom Kinde aus* (starting with the child), project methods, etc. Some of these proposals have been put into practice, but in order to succeed have to be met by two prerequisites: competent and committed teachers on the one hand, and on the other resources, both material and cultural, i.e., interested parents. Common to all these reform efforts, documented by Cullert (1986) who played a leading role in the preparation of the curriculum for the Swedish comprehensive school in the 1960s, is to base school learning on the children's own experiences and to bring 'real life' into the classroom. The experience-based pedagogy was sometimes developed by teachers in the public elementary school, the *Volksschule*, for a long time the most common school. It was developed in order to bring about a teaching strategy that took care of the whole range of abilities and interests and was not confined to an academic élite.

Cullert, in his pedagogical memoirs, has given us much insight into the heavy task of establishing a curriculum with the aim of catering to the needs of children at the level above the traditional 6-year elementary school and to make the curriculum oriented more towards 'real life' by cross-disciplinary integration, time concentration and project orientation. The reformers had to fight against traditions with a heavy momentum. It was like trying to turn around a supertanker and perform the manoeuvre in a short time.

The prolonged stay in school means it can offer young people the guidance and support that helps them build up competences needed to cope with the actual and future situations. To use an expression coined by Hartmut von Hentig (1987) and applied in his *Laborschule* (laboratory school) in Bielefeld, Germany: at the center of school pedagogy should be 'experiential learning.'

The task of providing entire age groups with a large variety of intellectual skills and interests with meaningful experiential learning poses a real challenge to secondary school pedagogy and runs against certain current demands from inside and outside school. The rising costs and the misgivings about what the schools are achieving have inspired demands for 'back to basics' teaching. It is maintained that the school should concentrate on what it is traditionally good at, namely the inculcation of book learning. Other kinds of learning that are important for the education of citizens should be taken care of by other institutions, such as the family, the church, the media and the workplace. This conception of division of labor between the school and the other institutions is based on the assumption that the other institutions are able and equipped to perform their tasks successfully as they have been in the past. But, as pointed out above, institutions, not least the family, have changed. Both parents are increasingly working outside the home and children are early into institutions at an early age, such as day-care centers, kindergartens and preschools. After class hours in the regular schools, school children increasingly spend the afternoon in youth centers before they can go home and join their parents. Publicly or privately organized leisure time activities take up a considerable part of children's spare time. The rest is television.

Thus the school is simply forced to shoulder educative tasks which were previously prerogatives of parents and/or grandparents. Such a development must necessarily have repercussions on school pedagogy. The school cannot limit its task to the transfer of a certain body of well-structured, textbook-based information. It must widen the scope of its tasks by opening up to the world outside the school. When the major role of education was catered for by the extended family and the community, the school could make a virtue of its particular strength, namely systematizing and categorizing the world outside school and conveying verbally to the pupils how things were 'out there,' even though experiential learning provided by the home and the community served as a counterweight.

What is required in order to make schooling a meaningful experience is to bring this world outside the school into the classroom and base teaching on students' experiences. This also implies the enlisting of help from people other than professional teachers. Every adult with experiences to share as a holder of an occupation and—not least—as an active citizen is a potential pedagogue.

Concluding Observations

As a social scientist for more than 40 years I have been involved in policy-oriented research connected with educational reform and planning (Husén, 1988). One general lesson learned, particularly from follow-ups of futurological studies, is that even with the best intentions things can 'go wrong' due to either originally unrecognized or unforeseen circumstances. Institutional development easily deviates from the lines drawn up by the intentions of policymakers and planners. In 1985 the Department of Political Science of the University of Uppsala, in honor of Ragnar Edenman, Swedish Minister of Education 1956–67, organized a seminar on the implementation of educational reforms. Particular attention was paid to the comprehensive school reform of the 1950s and early 1960s and the university reform of the late 1950s, both launched during Edenman's time as a Minister. In particular, school reform was launched under the banner of bringing about greater equality of opportunity with the ultimate goal of bringing about a more equal society without the traditional economic and status gaps between social strata. By abolishing the parallel system at the secondary level and by bringing young people from all strata together under the same roof, more equality should be secured. Reality far from matched the rhetoric. In an increasingly meritocratic high-technology society, where formal education has become the democratic substitute for inherited wealth and privilege, there are some who are born to more educated and education-minded parents than others and who more easily take the lead in terms of more prestigious and well-paid positions.

This was by and large not foreseen when the reforms were launched. Nor did we foresee the repercussions on the school as an institution, which catered for 100 per cent of the teenagers, of the changing structure and role of the family. Neither did we then, during an era of full employment, foresee the repercussions on the school that would come from the difficulties young people have in finding jobs to support themselves.

In reforming and planning schools for the future we should not forget that the school is part and parcel of society at large. The educational system alone cannot change society. It is rather the other way around.

In planning the schools for the beginning of the next century, which is virtually upon us, we must try to read and interpret carefully the writing on the wall which means we should try to study and diagnose the problems of *today* in order to avoid doing more of the same things tomorrow.

Those of us who have devoted time and efforts to studying the development of the school as an institution in modern society (see, e.g., Husén, 1979) have been struck by the increased bureaucratization. Sometimes one has the impression that bureaucrats, or rather technocrats, think that schools should be managed according to the same principles as manufacturing industries. Accordingly the school units have grown from the small red school houses to pedagogical factories in glass and concrete. This is a milieu in which pedagogical visionaries do not find themselves comfortably at home. The streamlining bureaucrats are more at ease here. But a proper balance must be achieved between those who advocate genuine educational values and those emphasizing administrative expediency. I do not for a moment believe in going back to the red school house, although

I feel much nostalgia for it from my own time in elementary school. But we should be wary of the dangers inherent in large-scale units. The major point in the message which I have tried to bring out in this presentation is that school pedagogy cannot avoid being strongly affected by fundamental changes in the surrounding society and that a mismatch can easily occur due to inherent institutional conservatism in the school.

References

Bell, D. (Ed.) (1967) Toward the year 2000; work in progress, *Daedalus*, XCVI, pp. 639–1226.

Coleman, J. S. and Husén, T. (1985) *Becoming Adult in a Changing Society* (Paris, OECD, also in French).

Cullert, B. (1986) *Med folkskolans pedagogik som riktmärke* (With the Pedagogy of the Elementary School as a Guide) (Stockholm, National Board of Education).

Härnqvist, K. (1961) *Individuella differenser och skoldifferentiering* (Individual Differences and School Differentiation) SOU 1960:13 (Stockholm, Government Printing Office).

Hentig, H. von (1987) *'Humanisierung'—eine verschämte Rückkehr zur Pädagogik* (Stuttgart, Klett-Cotta).

Husén, T. (1962) *Problems of Differentiation in Swedish Compulsory Schooling* (Stockholm, Scandinavian University Books).

Husén, T. (1971) *Utbildning år 2000* (Education in the Year 2000) (Stockholm, Bonniers).

Husén, T. (1974) *Talent, Equality and Meritocracy* (The Hague, Martinus Nijhoff).

Husén, T. (1979) *The School in Question* (London, Oxford University Press) (in seven languages).

Husén, T. (1981) *Present Trends in Education and Their Main Determinants* (Stockholm, International Institute of Education, University of Stockholm, Report No. 49).

Husén, T. (1986) *The Learning Society Revisited* (Oxford, Pergamon Press).

Husén, T. (1988) *Skolreformerna och forskningen* (The School Reforms and Research) (Stockholm, Verbum Gothia).

Kahn, H. and Weiner, A. J. (1967) *The Year 2000* (New York, Macmillan).

Teichler, U. (1976) *Das Dilemma der modernien Bildungsgesellschaft* (The Dilemma of the Modern Learning Society) (Stuttgart, Klett).

II

Research

Introduction

EDUCATIONAL RESEARCH, at least in Europe, came of age and had a break-through as a separate scholarly field during the first two decades after the Second World War. Demand for educational researchers and their 'products' arose because of a boom which occurred due to educational reforms and enrollment explosions in many countries, not to mention the need for research in planning and building of national systems of education in Third World countries. Educational researchers were expected to provide a knowledge base for structural and curricular reforms. Resources made available for commissioned and proposed research grew rapidly, particularly in the 'golden' sixties when the economies went through a period of expansion and education was espoused as a main vehicle for economic development. Expectations about what educational research would be able to deliver in terms of policy advice and improvement of classroom practices were running high. These expectations were not always met. The ensuing frustration tended, in some places, to reduce public support for education, a setback that education shared with other kinds of social science research. This inspired exercises in self-criticism with two kinds of questions asked. First, what is the proper role of research, and the researcher, *vis-à-vis* policymakers and practitioners? Second, what research paradigms are appropriate and adequate in dealing with the problems raised by the two categories of users of research? These are the questions taken up in the first of the three chapters in this section of the book.

Notes

[1]Published in *Interchange*, Vol. 19. No. 1. (Spring 1988) 2–12. Also published in Spanish in I. Dendaluce (Ed.) *Aspectos metodológicos de la investigación educativa* (Madrid: Narcea 1988).

[2]Paper presented at the Annual Conference on Education at the Universidad Interamericana in Puerto Rico 1985.

[3]Paper presented at the 1984 Symposium of the Nordic Association for the Study of Education in Developing Countries in Stockholm, September 1984.

6

Research Paradigms in Education

An Introduction to a Difficult Issue

BEFORE DISCUSSING what in the post-Kuhnian era of philosophy of science are referred to as 'research paradigms in education,' it would seem appropriate to try to delineate education as a field of inquiry. When William James gave his famous 'Talks to Teachers on Psychology,' he was keen to point out that education is not a science but an art:

> I say that you make a great, a very great mistake, if you think that psychology, being the science of the mind's laws, is something from which you can deduce definite programs and schemes and methods of instruction for immediate schoolroom use. Psychology is a science, and teaching is an art, and sciences never generate arts directly out of themselves. An intermediary inventive mind must make the application, by using its originality. (1899, pp. 7–8)

Depending upon the criteria employed in defining an area of study as a science, we may or may not dispute James's dictum. I for one am inclined to agree with him. But we can all agree that education as a field of research and study (as defined by the *International Encyclopedia of Education: Research and Studies*, for example) is far from being a clear-cut, well-defined, and delimited discipline, such as physics or history. A cursory look at the entries and the index in the *Encyclopedia* (Husén and Postlethwaite, 1985) or in textbooks presenting the so-called foundations of education immediately conveys a highly kaleidoscopic picture. Scholarly activities in education take place in many different disciplines and university departments. Some of these activities, such as studies of the history and philosophy of education, belong to the humanities. Others, like educational sociology and educational psychology, belong to the behavioral and social sciences.

Education as a field of study, although not necessarily of research, was first introduced at German universities in the late eighteenth century. The first chair in education was established at the University of Halle in the 1780s, although for a long time there were very few chairs in the field (Husén, 1983). Courses in education, offered to prospective secondary

59

school teachers, consisted in a philosophical grounding in the art of teaching. Competence in teaching, however, continued to be achieved by practice teaching following graduation from university. In some countries, notably France, education as a field of study was not admitted at all to the universities, and there was no empirical research anywhere. On the whole, education had great difficulty in being acknowledged as a proper academic field of inquiry. It tended to be at the bottom of the academic pecking order. An example from my home country illustrates this point.

Around the turn of this century, leaders of the Swedish elementary schools association demanded that chairs in educational psychology be established at the Swedish universities. A strong motive for their insistence was that the establishment of scholarly studies in the art of teaching would be a great step forward in the professionalization of teaching and would thereby enhance the status of elementary school teachers, who were trained at seminaries or normal schools and not at the universities. Secondary school teachers (who did attend the universities, studying in particular disciplines) believed that teaching did not require any academic grounding. In France, for example, graduates from the university went straight to teaching. It was assumed that if one had acquired a high level of competence in a particular discipline then by implication one would become a good teacher in that field.

When the first man to hold the professorial chair in education at the University of Uppsala was to be inaugurated, the Rector of the University issued an invitation accompanied by a booklet in which he gave the background of the establishment of the chair, as was the custom at the University before welcoming a new colleague. The Rector, who held the chair of the history of literature, commented on the new chair:

From what has been said it is evident that Professor Hammer is going to occupy a position subject to controversy. On the one hand education has been regarded as being almost the most important of all disciplines of our time. On the other hand, one has feared that interest in the *methods* of teaching would have a detrimental effect on the strict knowledge which after all has to be mastered by the prospective teacher. When the university now extends its good wishes to the new professor they imply that Professor Hammer will be able by his achievements to bring these fears to nought. (Segerstedt, 1983, p. 60)

The new chairholder could, indeed, have been greeted more generously!

I was reminded of this story when for the first time I visited Teachers College, Columbia University, in the early 1950s. This institution (founded in 1887 to provide graduate studies and promote research in education) is located on 120th Street, which divides the complex of buildings making up Columbia University from the College. Pointing to the street, the Dean of Graduate Studies at the College said, 'You know, this is the broadest street in the world.'

In the late nineteenth century, psychology was established at some universities as an experimental and empirical discipline. The first psychological laboratory was set up in Leipzig in 1879. The following decade saw a breakthrough in empirical studies in child development—by Wilhelm Preyer in Europe and by Stanley Hall, the pioneer of American psychology. Hall, who studied in Germany in the 1870s, became head of the first department of psychology of the first American graduate school, at Johns Hopkins, in the early 1880s. He founded several journals in psychology and education and, as President of Clark University, was a prolific writer involved in a large number of research studies. Most remarkable of these was his monumental *Adolescence* (1904), based to a large extent on data obtained from the extensive administration of questionnaires.

By the turn of the century psychology based on experiments and systematic observations began to be conceived as *the* scientific foundation of studies in education *par préférence*. Experimental studies in education began. In 1907, Wundt's student Ernst Meumann published his *Einführung in die experimentelle Pädagogik* (*Introduction to Experimental Pedagogy*) in three large volumes.

Three fields of study in psychology were expected to elucidate educational problems: (1) psychology of child development, (2) psychology of learning, and (3) psychology of individual differences. In all three of these fields there were breakthroughs at the turn of the century. I have already made reference to Hall and child development. Clara and William Stern in Hamburg and, later, Charlotte and Karl Bühler in Vienna and Alfred Binet in France provided a basis for experimental and/or observational studies. In America, Edward Lee Thorndike was the great pioneer. We are all acquainted with his dictum that whatever exists is there to some amount and therefore can be measured.

Education as a scholarly pursuit was for a long time identified with educational psychology, that is, psychology applied to educational problems. Even in the late 1930s and early 1940s, when I took my doctoral studies and prepared for a professorship, we never talked about 'educational' research, only about 'psycho-educational' research. There were no separate chairs in education in Sweden until about 1950, but the subject was taught by professors in psychology and education who headed institutes of psychology. In the 1940s I applied for a chair in psychology, and in the 1950s I became the second president of the Swedish Psychological Association, an organization I had been instrumental in founding.

For a long time problems in education were conceived of as purely didactic or pedagogic: *what* to teach and *how* to teach it. Developmental psychology was expected to tell educators what kind of subject matter the child was able to absorb and what kind of learning material would be compatible with the child's level of development. The psychology of learning and of individual differences could tell educators what kind of methods would be most suitable.

But the range of disciplines bearing on education has widened, and so has the perspective on educational problems. Changes occurring in the social sciences generally had strong repercussions on educational research. Its problems were conceived of in a larger context by sociologists, anthropologists, and economists. The conditions of education outside the classroom, such as the home and society at large, began to be studied. Reforms of the structure of the school system and the curricula also required a broader perspective than that which psychology could provide. Quests for greater equality of opportunity initiated studies of how social background affects educational attainments (Husén, 1975). Education came to be seen as an investment in national development, a perspective that gave rise to studies on how education provides economic benefits to both the individual and the society. The growth of aid to developing countries inspired studies of how education is related to national development (Fägerlind and Saha, 1983).

At many American universities, pedagogy and didactics dominated departments of education until the early 1950s. Even though comparative education courses and 'foundation' courses in the philosophy and sociology of education were given, educational psychology was the prominent and prestigious study. But at some leading institutions people began to realize that fruitful research in education had to be cross-disciplinary. This could be achieved by joint appointments in the department of education and another department, such as economics, sociology, or history. Thus at such universities as Chicago and Stanford (established leaders in educational research with strong graduate departments), economists, political scientists, and sociologists have over the last few decades worked both in their 'mother' disciplines and in the graduate department of education. At the University of Chicago, for example, the Center for Comparative Education served as a focal point for cross-disciplinary fertilization.

Politics of education, as well as policy studies in education, has been an emerging cross-disciplinary specialty, inspired by the increased efforts of national governments to promote educational research in order to extend the knowledge base for educational reform and for the bringing about of improvements in educational practice. This development has been strengthened by co-operation with political scientists and sociologists. Cases in point are James March at Stanford, Martin Trow at Berkeley, and Maurice Kogan at Brunel. I also have in mind some young political scientists in Sweden (notably Björn Wittrock and Rune Premfors) who have pioneered studies in higher education.

The Paradigm Problem

It is against this background sketch of the nature of education that we should examine the paradigm problem, a controversy that has loomed large both in the social sciences in general and in education in particular since the late 1960s. Research in education has grown enormously over the last few decades. Financial and institutional resources as well as the number of researchers involved and publications produced have multiplied exponentially. No wonder, then, that expectations about the achievements of educational research in helping to frame educational policy and improve educational practice have been running high, often beyond realistic limits. Under the impact of such expectations and the frustrations they create, the relationship between research and policy making in education has begun to be studied (Husén and Kogan, 1984).

A major breakthrough in the behavioral and social sciences took place after the Second World War. The role of these sciences fitted well into the conception of rationality and social engineering held by many policy-makers and leading educators. The so-called positivist research paradigm (whatever is meant by that misused term) dominated. The model that once provided the natural sciences with their experimental designs spread to education. According to the literature, the ideal for a classroom experiment on teaching was to assign students at random to experimental and control classes. One independent variable, a particular method of teaching, say, was manipulated. The effect on the dependent variable (for example, the amount of subject matter learned) was measured. Data were of value only if they were quantifiable and could be subjected to strict and sophisticated statistical analyses, particularly multivariate analysis. Only experimental designs allowed causal inferences of the sort that were part of what Karl Pearson (1892) referred to as the 'Grammar of Science,' that is, the natural sciences.

The next best strategy was survey research. Even though it did not allow strict causal inferences, it made it possible to identify which independent variables were relevant and to what extent they contributed to variation in the dependent variable. The large survey of equality of educational opportunity by Coleman *et al.* (1966) and the IEA cross-national surveys of achievements in mathematics and science (see Husén, 1979, and 'Special Issue,' 1987) are classic examples of this strategy.

At the bottom of the methdological pecking order were various qualitative approaches, such as ethnography and participant observation. These were tolerated only if they could be formalized so as to allow quantification.

Epistemological Background of the Problem

The reaction against the positivist paradigm came in the late 1960s through a confluence of various forces. The tension between basic epistemological conceptions was long-standing. As early as the 1890s,

Wilhelm Dilthey had advanced the notion that, in knowing, there are basic differences between the humanities and the natural sciences. The former aims at 'understanding' (*Verstehen*) and the latter at 'explaining' (*Erklären*). The Frankfurt school of critical philosophy (with Horkheimer and Adorno and, later, Habermas) took a critical attitude *vis-à-vis* the positivist approach in the social sciences and accused those who advocated that approach of conservatism. The very concept of knowledge was reassessed in the direction of what could be called an interactionist model. The researcher, his or her theory, and the 'reality' under study interacted. New approaches in looking at these realities were offered by the phenomenologists, such as Husserl and Heidegger. But we must remember also that the great expectations for the scientific method borrowed from the natural sciences were not met. Even the most elaborate classroom experiments or the most accurate quantitative surveys, like the IEA surveys or the Coleman equality study, left the interpreters of the findings uncertain and sometimes confused. Thus, fresh new approaches were needed.

The positivist, realist, quantitatively oriented paradigms have by no means gone undisputed, not even in the United States. On the contrary, this approach has been brought into question many times in recent years—not least of all in the *Educational Researcher*, organ of the American Educational Research Association. Without highlighting even the main points in this debate, let me say that there are those, such as Egon Guba (1978), who think that a more qualitative, interpretive, hermeneutic, and 'naturalistic' paradigm can supplement the positivistic. But there are also those, not necessarily of a positivist conviction, who maintain that 'never the twain shall meet.'

Multifaceted human behavior, with all its context-bound subtle nuances, cannot adequately be captured within the epistemological and methodological framework of neo-positivism. Therefore, symbolic interactionism can serve as a more adequate model for the study of the processes in education. Instead of employing the hypothetico-deductive paradigm with its quantification and search for clear-cut causes, one should try to describe the complex reciprocal social interactions.

Behind the two approaches are, of course, two different ways of defining the 'reality' somewhere 'out there' and what should be regarded as 'valid' knowledge. There are two different epistemologies in the social sciences. According to the quantitatively oriented, realist tradition, the world 'out there' can be described as it 'really is.' According to the other approach, what we learn about the world is filtered through our senses. Therefore, scientific knowledge does not reflect the real nature of the world. In this idealist, interpretive approach, social reality is mind-dependent and, in a way, mind-constructed. 'Truth was ultimately a matter of socially and historically conditioned agreement' (Smith and Heshusius, 1986).

As pointed out above, the latter conception is by no means an invention of the last few years. It goes back to Dilthey in the late nineteenth century. Dilthey saw the interpretive or hermeneutical approach as germane to the cultural and moral sciences. Human and social phenomena are subject to intentionality; therefore, it is not possible to separate what is investigated from the investigator. The researcher is enmeshed in the social reality of which he or she is a part. The natural scientist observes what is happening 'out there' in the cyclotron or in the test tube. The investigator of human and social phenomena arrives at knowledge by 'inner experience' with what in the German philosophical literature has been referred to as *Einfühlung*.

The crucial point here, of course, concerns who is to check the validity of the knowledge arrived at. This depends on how truth is defined. For those using the quantitative approach, 'truth' is defined by the things 'out there.' If the validity is disputed, one has only to look at the 'facts,' preferably the quantitatively established facts. But this implies a quantitative inquiry. Certain techniques are epistemologically more justified, or privileged, than others.

The qualitative, interpretive approach does not accept that any techniques should *a priori* be epistemologically privileged. Reality is idealist-oriented, that is, reality is mind-dependent and no techniques can claim epistemological privilege. 'Reality is made rather than found.' Validity of a certain knowledge depends very much on consensus among interpreters.

This business of validity is, of course, crucial. It has been maintained that the solution lies in 'what works,' the major touchstone of pragmatism. There is something in this in the sense that research in education, as pointed out earlier, is conducted with a certain *purpose* in mind. Usually there is a quest for knowledge that can serve as a basis for policy action or change in classroom practice.

Can the 'twain meet'? In a recent article, Smith and Heshusius (1986) argue that 'the claim of compatibility and the call for co-operation between quantitative and qualitative inquiry cannot be sustained' (p. 4). I would like to emphasize that the *purpose* of the inquiry determines which approaches will turn out to be most fruitful.

The Objective of Research Determines the Paradigm

Let me repeat the point made above, one that appears rather self-evident. The strategy or paradigm one opts for depends largely upon the *objective* one has in mind for the research one undertakes. If the purpose is to assess the level of competence achieved in, say, mathematics in a given school, region, or entire nation, then the quantitatively oriented survey approach would be the obvious choice. If the purpose is to monitor the effects of a school reform, to assess which students in a given country have been able to achieve according to international standards, or to compare students in different school systems or countries, then the researcher can hardly avoid certain techniques of quantification, such as administering standardized achievement tests to representative samples of students. The alternative is to rely on folklore about the relative advantages and failings of national systems of education, a knowledge based at best on first-hand impressions by competent visitors, at worst, on second-hand impressions or downright prejudices.

Let me give one example of this approach to research. When I served as Chair of the National Commission on Education in Botswana in the mid-1970s, it was decided to assess the level of competence among primary school leavers in that country. English was used as the medium of instruction from the third school year, and members of the Commission suspected that quite a lot of confusion was caused by the switch from the mother tongue to a completely different language before the pupils were literate in their mother tongue. We tested reading comprehension at the end of primary school (grade 7) with reading items in English adapted to the indigenous culture. We found that on average the students read at what would be a second-grade level in Britain or the United States. Quite a few were unable to read such simple sentences as 'Peter has a dog.' The evidence we presented to policymakers in Botswana convinced them that the switch from mother tongue to English would have to be postponed. Students would have to be made literate in their mother tongue, at least in a rudimentary way, before a foreign language could be used as the medium of instruction. (And the teachers' English would have to improve, as well.)

In cases such as this, only the survey approach can provide overriding parameters, such as statistics about achievement levels and distribution of competence. But such an approach cannot tell us how the pedagogical subtleties constituting the infrastructure of instruction bring about a certain level of competence. Knowledge about the pedagogical background can be obtained by observing and interviewing teachers and students in a number of classrooms, that is, by employing what is often referred to as ethnographic data collection (which, by the way, can sometimes be quantified). This is what we did in the IEA classroom environment study, which was inspired by the shortcomings of the pure survey approach.

A second main point pertaining to the adequacy of paradigms is that quantitative and qualitative paradigms are complementary. It is not possible to arrive at any valid information about the level of achievement in, say, science in a given school or school system only by visiting classrooms where science instruction is going on and collecting impressions. Even a highly experienced science teacher would not be able to provide information that would allow accurate inferences about the quality of outcomes of science teaching in an entire system or nation. Sample surveys are necessary here. But they are by far too superficial when it comes to accounting for what is behind the differences between school systems or nations. Here qualitative information of different kinds is required.

In addition to ethnographic techniques one has to enlist the help of educational historians, philosophers, and anthropologists who represent other research strategies than the quantitatively oriented survey one, be it called positivist or not. I had just spent some time in China discussing the Chinese IEA study in science when I ran into Sir Joseph Needham in an antiquarian bookshop in Shanghai. Sir Joseph had just finished, if I remember correctly, the eighth volume in his series on the history of Chinese science education. He would certainly have been the one to tell us about the adequacy of the test items used in assessing the competence of Chinese secondary school students. To be sure, a social anthropologist, such as Professor Chie Nakane of the University of Tokyo, would be in the position to help the IEA researchers explain the particular drive and motivation found among Japanese and Chinese students, both in Asia and in the United States. As a Visiting Professor at the University of California, Berkeley some time ago, I mentioned to the President of the University how struck I was by the high proportion of Asian students in attendance. He confirmed my observation by saying that one third of the students were of Asian background, a remarkable number given that people of Asian descent accounted for only some 5 to 6 per cent of California's total population. To explain this is, indeed, a challenging task for social anthropologists and sociologists. Differential psychologists and educational psychologists with their arsenal of quantitative and statistical tools are not very useful here, but, as pointed out above, their role is to establish certain basic parameters.

The Problem of 'Methodological Colonialism'

The issue of paradigmatic adequacy is not only an epistemological but also an ethical one. It can be stated succinctly like this: 'Who is going to tell whom what to do?' Let me illustrate this by an experience from the international scene. As part of China's so-called modernization, an upgrading of science teaching at both the secondary and the university levels came into focus. The then Minister of Education of the People's Republic visited Sweden in order to establish co-operation with Swedish institutions. Since the IEA International Secretariat was located in Stockholm, he expressed interest in learning about the IEA surveys. He explained that he wanted science competence among Chinese secondary school students to be evaluated according to the same standards as those used in Japan, Britain, and the United States. What should I have told him? Should I have said that he did not know what was best for his own people? That it was absurd to evaluate science competence in China with tests devised to a large extent by and for people from the Western industrialized countries? That he could not fairly make comparisons between them and the Chinese?

Researchers from countries with a tradition and a background of systematic research in the social sciences and with impressive resources have an advantage over those from countries with a short research tradition and fewer resources when it comes to the planning and implementation of comparative studies requiring a uniform research methodology, such as the IEA research requires. The problem is further aggravated by the fact that most Third World researchers have been trained in Europe or the United States.

Research in education, as we encounter it in the literature, has until recently been conducted almost entirely in Europe, America, and in industrial countries outside the northern hemisphere, such as Australia. In planning the *International Encyclopedia of Education*, I attempted to discover where scholarly studies in education since about 1950 had been conducted and published. The United States alone accounted for more than half of the world's production of scholarly monographs, papers, reports, and so on in education. This was no surprise, given the number of Americans engaged in full-time educational research. The American Educational Research Association has for decades had a membership of several thousand. The present number is about 10,000, the majority of whom are active researchers with advanced degrees and based at university institutions. There are more educational researchers in the US than in all the European countries together.

Recently, the Canadian IDRC and the World Bank reviewed the resources and quality of educational research in the developing countries. In the whole of Africa, there are less than 100 people actively engaged in full-time educational research, that is, less than one per cent of the task force in research in the United States. Furthermore, the great majority of those engaged in research in Africa, Asia, and Latin America have been trained in the United States and Europe.

This lack of balance between the industrial and the non-industrial countries in terms of staff and other resources is, of course, a matter of concern. Connected with it is another issue, that of the adequacy of the European-American research paradigms for use in developing countries. Critical voices have been raised, particularly against the classical, natural-science oriented, positivist paradigm that has dominated social science research in the affluent countries during the twentieth century.

Sometimes the affluent countries have been accused (mostly by their own researchers) of exercising a kind of 'methodological colonialism.'

The main issue here is whether we can talk about research paradigms that are more adequate for developing than for industrialized societies. If we consider the natural sciences, the immediate answer is 'no.' We can hardly talk about African physics as opposed to European physics any more than we can talk about German physics as opposed to French physics. But in the social sciences the situation is somewhat different. Here we are so close to policy and social action, where values are deeply involved. We need to consider the different kinds of knowledge gained by different research approaches.

In discussing the transferability of research paradigms in education from First World to Third World countries we should consider that social knowledge has certain culture-bound parameters. I was reminded of this a few years ago when I listened to a presentation by my colleague Ed Gordon (1984), Professor at Yale University, on 'Social Science and the Ethno-Cultural Experience.' He pointed out that a given variable may take on a different meaning and have a different impact on people in different cultural and ethnic contexts. This has to be considered in both cross-cultural and multicultural research in education. Gordon made the point that we have rushed too quickly from description to analysis, causal or not, and he made a plea for a more hermeneutic approach.

But is it possible to solve this problem by simply relinquishing the entire research tradition in the so-called developed countries and opting instead for indigenous methods of a more qualitative nature? A colleague who expressed concern about what he perceived as 'methodological colonialism' on the part of the First World was once asked the question I just posed. He replied, 'That is the price we would have to pay.' He was on the faculty of a leading American university. It appears to me that the logical consequence of his answer would have been to relinquish his role as a teacher and supervisor of graduate students from Third World countries enrolled at his university.

The Unity of Educational Research

It has been said that the various research paradigms in education—the empirical-positivist, the hermeneutic or phenomenological, and the ethnographic-anthropological—are complementary to each other. John Keeves (1988) has talked about the 'unity of educational research.' He contends that there is only one paradigm but many approaches which can be seen as complementary to each other. Many, perhaps most, problems in education can certainly be better investigated when examined by means of different approaches. What goes on in a school or a school system can be studied in many different ways. The teaching-learning process can be observed and video-recorded. The observations can be quantified and the data analyzed by means of advanced statistical techniques. Content can be studied by examining it in light of a particular national tradition and the objectives underlying curriculum construction. Both the teaching-learning process and its outcomes can be studied in a cross-national comparative and/or a longitudinal perspective.

The implication of what I am saying here is, again, that the *purpose* of a given study determines the nature of the approach. The ultimate purpose of any research endeavor in education is to arrive at knowledge that can be used for *action*, be it a policy action or a change of classroom practice. Thus, the way we go about studying a given problem depends to a large extent on *what kind of knowledge* we want to gain by our research endeavors.

Let me illustrate this by means of the cross-national research studies I have been involved in for more than twenty-five years. These are the IEA surveys in mathematics and science. As I have indicated elsewhere (Husén, 1979), the cross-national, co-operative research known under the acronym IEA (International Association for the Evaluation of Educational Achievement) was originally initiated by a group of educational psychologists, most of them experts in educational measurement *and* testing. The cross-national research they launched was partially inspired by public concern about the quality of mathematics and science teaching as manifested in the quality of the technology of a given country. This quality was seen as a major determinant of the nation's competitiveness on the international market. (This, after all, was the time of Sputnik.)

We, the researchers, had two main purposes for the first IEA surveys in mathematics. We wanted to find out why students at the same age or grade level performed differently in different countries and how this variability was accounted for by home background, school resources, and teaching practices. The second, more implicit purpose, which was also the basis for the first, was to compare national systems of education in terms of average performance among students at certain age and grade levels in the system. Sometimes, in a derogatory way, we referred to this as the 'horse race' aspect of our surveys.

Irrespective of which of the two purposes predominated, the only feasible way of arriving at strict comparisons of student achievement was to test representative samples of students drawn from the various national student populations. To have sent a group of experienced (multilingual!) teachers to the various countries to observe what was happening in a very limited, and not necessarily representative, selection of classrooms would have resulted in a host of kaleidoscopic impressions, which could hardly be used for strict comparative purposes. Thus given the explicit and implicit purposes of our investigation, the only feasible strategy was an empirical, quantitative, and statistically descriptive one.

As anticipated, we found a great range among national systems of education in terms of average performance, as well as between schools and, of course, between students. It should be pointed out that the range in average performance among industrial countries was rather small compared to the huge difference between industrial and non-industrial countries. Furthermore, the between-school variance compared to between-student variance was small in some countries (in Sweden, 10 per cent of student variance), whereas it was much larger in other countries (in India, about 80 per cent of the between-student variance). In our attempts to explain the between-nation, between-school, and between-student variance, we set out to develop a theoretical model, an 'input-output' model. Such a model was expected to guide multivariate analyses of how factors related to home, school resources, and instruction accounted for the variances under study.

As I have spelled out elsewhere (Husén, 1979), we were not very successful in these analytical endeavors. We had developed good measurement instruments—carefully devised and standardized achievement tests that were fair and on the whole cross-nationally valid. There was no reason to dispute the assumption that between-country differences in average scores were 'true' reflections of between-nation differences in, say, mathematical competence among students. But why, for instance, did Japanese 14 and 18 year olds perform much better than their age mates in Europe and America? Or why did Swedish 10 year olds perform at least as well in reading as British 10 year olds in spite of the fact that the Swedish children entered school one to two years later than the British? How did it come about that Japanese schools with classes of forty to fifty children 'produced' on average better results in terms of mean scores than Swedish classes with twenty to twenty-five children?

Conclusive answers to questions like these can hardly be provided by large-scale surveys based on test scores and replies to questionnaires. Other approaches are called for. Take the Japanese case. When the First International Mathematics Study (Husén, 1967) revealed the high level of competence among schoolchildren in Japan, various explanations were advanced, none of which could be firmly supported by the multivariate analyses. I suggested on one occasion that we should identify a few Japanese schools which scored very high and some which scored very low and then conduct comparative classroom observations. This could give us some leads in accounting for the high level of performance of Japanese students. Such an approach is initially a task for researchers trained in ethnographic methods, a task primarily for social anthropologists.

What IEA measured at best were certain *cognitive outcomes* of school learning, although not even the entire cognitive spectrum was covered and mapped out by standardized tests. The IEA test arsenal also included some attitude tests, measuring, for example, attitudes toward mathematics and schooling in general. But what about major outcomes referred to as 'affective'—outcomes having to do with personality development, character formation, ability to co-operate and to shoulder responsibility (the objectives emphasized in most curricular documents)? Examination of these is a task for direct, more or less participant observation and hermeneutic interpretation.

Thus the methodological approaches (whether or not we want to refer to them as *paradigms*) are not necessarily in conflict with each other. Depending upon our aims in seeking knowledge we can arrive at a multi-faceted picture of the problem we want to elucidate by taking different methodological routes. In trying to come to grips with educational problems we are faced in the end with value problems. What kind of policy do we want to pursue? What kind of reform or change in educational practice do we want to achieve? In cases where we emphasize improvement we are not well served by a paradigm that purportedly aims at 'value-free' information.

The received 'grammar' of scientific inquiry has been put in question. The 'post-positivist paradigm' has been degraded. But the criticism of empirical positivism with all its quantitative and statistical tools has fortunately not led to the throwing of the baby out with the bathwater. Even if knowledge is conceived as action-related and dependent upon the purpose of the study, there is, indeed, still something to be gained from the 'established' approaches.

References

Coleman, J. S., Campbell, E. Q., Hobson, C. J., McPartland, J., Mood, A. M., Weinfeld, F. D., and York, R. L. (1966) *Equality of educational opportunity*. Washington, DC: US Department of Health, Education and Welfare, Office of Education.
Fägerlind, I. and Saha, L. (1983) *Education and national development*. Oxford: Pergamon Press.
Gordon, E. (1984) *Social science and the ethno-cultural experience*. Paper presented at a meeting of the US National Academy of Education, Chicago.
Guba, E. (1978) *Toward a methodology of naturalistic inquiry in educational evaluation*. Los Angeles: University of California, Center for Study in Evaluation.
Hall, G. S. (1905) *Adolescence: Its psychology and its relations to physiology, anthropology, sociology, sex, crime, religion and education*. New York: D. Appleton.
Husén, T. (Ed.) (1967) *International study of achievements in mathematics*. New York: Wiley.
Husén, T. (1975) *Social influences on educational attainment*. Paris: OECD/CERI.
Husén, T. (1979) An international research venture in retrospect: The IEA surveys. *Comparative Education Review*, 23(3), 371–385.
Husén, T. (1983) Educational research and the making of policy in education: An international perspective. *Minerva*, 21(1), 81–100.
Husén, T. and Kogan, M. (Eds.) (1984) *Educational research and policy: How do they relate?* Oxford: Pergamon Press.
Husén, T. and Postlethwaite, T. N. (Eds.) (1985) *International encyclopedia of education: Research and studies*. Oxford: Pergamon Press.
James, W. (1899) *Talks to teachers on psychology*. London: Longmans, Green and Co.
Keeves, J. (1988) The Unity of Educational Research. *Interchange*, Vol. 19, No. 1, pp. 14–30.
Pearson, K. (1892) *The grammar of science*. London: Adam and Charles Black.

Segerstedt, T. (1983) *Universitet i Uppsala från 1952 till 1977* (The University of Uppsala from 1952 to 1977). Uppsala.

Smith, J. K. and Heshusius, L. (1986) Closing down the conversation: The end of the quantitative-qualitative debate among educational inquirers. *Educational Researcher*, 15(1), 4–12.

Special Issue on the IEA Research. (1987) *Comparative Education Review*, 31(1).

7

What Is Quality in Education?

Background

CONCERNS ABOUT the quality of education in a particular country tend to be aired in connection with educational reforms, particularly those of a structural nature. Thus, the introduction of comprehensive secondary education on a small and local scale in Britain in the 1950s and 1960s and on a national scale in Sweden in the 1950s and 1960s gave rise to a vivid controversy about the standards achieved in the 'new' type of school as compared to the 'old' one (Husén, 1962). A rather confused debate followed, at least in Sweden, since very few, if anybody, really cared to define what concretely should be meant by 'standards.' The concerns in the case of Sweden had to do with the standards achieved after the major reform as compared to those before the reform. The critics maintained that the standards had been lowered by the broadening of access to furthergoing education and, in particular, by keeping an unsorted or undifferentiated student body in the same classroom. One could here refer to the so-called Black Papers in Britain (Cox and Dyson, 1969 and 1970).

Reform proponents usually did not deny that the average achievement level had gone down but pointed to certain social gains, such as the elimination of the social bias, by making furthergoing education available to all young people. Another issue, which loomed large, was whether 'standards' should be defined solely by cognitive achievements or if a broader spectrum of educational objectives having to do with character formation and personality development should be considered, and how. Those who are against changes usually tend to favor the more narrow definition of objectives, whereas the protagonists of reforms tend to favor a wider definition of evaluation criteria.

In the debate whether standards are falling or not, an issue which seems to be inevitable after every major school reform, reference is usually made to other countries either because they have not changed their systems and have thereby been able to maintain high standards or because they have, indeed, changed and thereby been able to achieve something better. Experiences of a general practical nature or research findings from the same country have sometimes been used both in favor and against certain reform proposals in another country. This was the case with Sweden, how its experiences were interpreted in the mid-1960s in both Britain and the Federal Republic of Germany (Husén, 1983). In Britain, the then Minister of Education Anthony Crosland had far-reaching plans for comprehensivization of secondary education (Judge, 1984). He used Sweden as a good example, whereas the conservatives behind the Black Papers used it as a deterrent. In the Federal Republic of Germany, members of the *Bildungsrat* (Education Council), short of time to sponsor any domestic research, referred to the so-called Stockholm survey on the effects of comprehensivization and grouping as supporting the idea of a *Gesamtschule* (comprehensive school), whereas other members interpreted the survey as an indication of a failure of the comprehensive structure (Becker, 1979).

The massive involvement of governments during the 1960s in improving the quality of education gave rise to demands for accountability in terms of quality. A case in point is the programs sponsored by the Federal Government in the United States during the Johnson administration. But these programs, such as Title 1 in the Elementary and Secondary Education Act of 1965, with provisions for school children in poverty areas, and Title 4, which funded a vastly expanded research and development program in education, called for evaluation. Massive attempts were made to evaluate Head Start and other major programs. Most notable among these attempts is the Follow Through project. Rivlin and Timpane (1975), from the vantage point of being government employees during that period, dealt with problems associated with planned changes and their evaluation.

But concerns in the highly industrialized countries about the relative 'standard' or 'quality' achieved in different national systems of education have also been inspired by international competition, not least between major economic and military powers. In the wake of the Cold War in the 1950s and, not least, in the wake of the launching of Sputnik in 1957, criticisms, not to say disenchantment, began to be aired in the United States about the lack of 'intellectual rigor' particularly in secondary schools. Already in the early 1950s representatives of American universities had begun to subject the high school to strong criticism. Typical cases of this are the books by Lynd (1953) under the title *Quackery in the Public Schools* or by Bestor (1953) under the no less provocative title *Educational Wastelands: A Retreat from Learning in the Public Schools*.

At the same time Hyman Rickover, naval officer and the man behind the nuclear-powered submarines, found that the engineers employed in his projects did not have the proper grounding, in the first place in mathematics and science but in other subjects as well. He took a highly committed part in the debate on the quality of American education and was called upon to give testimony before the US Congress. In connection with this he began to take interest in comparing American and European secondary education. He referred to the high standards achieved in the (highly selective) German *Gymnasium* as something that should be emulated. Typically, the book in which he collected his articles and testimonies about American education carried the title *Education and Freedom* (Rickover, 1959).

Both in North America and in Europe the debate on the quality of secondary education had a strong impact on the development of comparative education as a field of scholarly inquiry. Large-scale cross-national surveys, in which attempts were made to measure quantitatively the standards in various countries, such as the IEA surveys (Husén, 1967), would have been inconceivable without such a background. Instead of sweeping statements based on subjective impressions about the relative level of competence achieved by students, objective tests were devised and standardized in co-operation with researchers, from various countries. The group of researchers, who later organized themselves into the International Association for the Evaluation of Educational Achievement (IEA) conducted a feasibility study in twelve countries between 1959 and 1961 and were able to show that data could be collected, processed, and analyzed uniformly so as to arrive at an empirical basis for cross-country comparisons (Foshay, 1962).

Under the impact of Sputnik, delegations of American educators, not least comparative educators (e.g., Bereday *et al.*, 1960) began to visit the Soviet Union in order to learn how one managed to bring students to a level in science and technology that could account for an achievement such as Sputnik.

The next stage of heightened interest in cross-national comparisons came during the international recession in the late 1970s when some nations were doing better in international trade, particularly with manufactured goods, than others. In the United States there were concerns about the successes by Japan and Taiwan as compared with the defeats of its own industry which was hit even in the Silicon Valley. This inspired a series of comparative studies of curricula, teaching methods and student achievement in the countries mentioned. The academic underpinnings of high technology, where international competition was fierce, were identified as proper teaching (with competent teachers, enough periods per week and assigning enough homework to students) particularly in mathematics and science. In spite of high general unemployment there has on both sides of the Atlantic been a serious lack of adequately trained manpower in fields such as microelectronics and biotechnology. This has been blamed on deficient provisions by the schools in the subject areas, particularly in science and mathematics, at the basis of competencies in these fields.

A typical expression of the concerns about lack of relative competitive power and the tendency to blame it on the educational system was the appointment of the National Commission on Excellence in Education in the United States. Even more typically of how these problems are conceived is the title of the Commission's report 'A Nation at Risk: The Imperative for Educational Reform.'

A third set of circumstances which has inspired cross-national comparisons of what schools achieve in terms of student competencies is related to the rapidly growing internationalization of higher education. An overriding problem here is how to establish international equivalents of requirements for leaving examinations from upper secondary school in various subjects. One approach to this was the so-called International Baccalauréat (Halls, 1985), a project established in the late 1960s where a number of secondary schools joined forces to compare requirements and to have subject area experts look at examination papers. The standards were defined in general, descriptive terms and not by mean scores on international tests, such as is the case in IEA surveys. Another aspect of the internationalization has to do with the rapidly growing number of students from developing countries at universities in Europe and North America. When it comes to sending graduate students abroad it becomes imperative to compare university departments in a given discipline in the various countries in order to send students overseas to the best departments in the respective fields.

Given the competition on the military and economic scenes, and the rising costs per student per year in the highly industrialized countries during a period of recession, it is not surprising to find a mounting concern, or even an obsession, with the *quality* achieved in school education. In some countries the per-pupil costs per annum have more than doubled in constant prices over the last two decades which, of course, raises such questions as 'Are the students twice as competent?' or 'Are they twice as happy and well behaved?' (Husén, 1979). The high priority given to the quality problem in the United States is reflected in the fact that the Reagan administration early made it a major policy issue. The National Commission on Excellence in Education was appointed to investigate the problem and come up with recommendations on how quality in American schools should be enhanced. The Commission, given its terms of reference, made it a major task to find out what American students were able to achieve in comparison with students in other highly industrialized countries, and invited testimonies and papers from researchers in comparative education, of whom I was one. (Husén, 1982) In April 1983 the Commission submitted its report with a long series of recommendations. In the United States, in addition to the National Commission, there have been more than 200 commissions and task forces at the state level which have dealt with the quality problems. State legislatures have followed several of their recommendations.

The Commission and other bodies were very much concerned about the lack of qualified teachers in certain subjects, such as science and mathematics. Liberal-arts bachelors have to an alarming degree become teachers in such subjects without adequate subject-matter preparation. Therefore the Commission assumed that teachers with better subject-matter preparation would improve classroom instruction in their respective fields and produce more competent students. More rigorous qualifying examinations were called for. Teachers should be better paid in order for the schools to compete with business and industry for good graduates.

The Commission furthermore recommended an increased number of hours of instruction in certain key subjects pointing out that in the United States the total amount of instruction is considerably lower than that in other comparable countries. Already one year after the report was published more than twenty states had legislated an increased load of instruction.

In the IEA study of French as a foreign language student competence in French was plotted against the amount of instruction given in terms of number of school years and number of hours. The plots between number of years and mean student achievement formed almost a straight line with the United States, usually with only two years of teaching French in high school, at the bottom, and Roumania with 5–6 years at the top (Carroll, 1975).

It should, however, be pointed out that the importance of time, as measured by number of years of instruction, number of hours per week and the number of hours spent on homework, varies a lot between subject areas. Time for *practice* both in school and at home is crucial in skill subjects, particularly those where the student starts from scratch, such as in learning foreign languages. The IEA study of French mentioned above is a case in point.

In other subjects, where the content relates to experiences which are made both before entering school and during school age outside the school, the amount of formal teaching is only weakly correlated with level of achievement which is also evidenced by the IEA surveys in correlational comparisons across countries (Passow *et al.*, 1976).

Homework is one factor which in many surveys stands out as important. In the IEA surveys it accounted for more of the between-student variance than other school-related variables. Comparisons between Japan and the United States showed that homework, which was much more frequent in Japan than in the United States, partly accounted for the higher standards among Japanese students.

What Should We Mean by Quality?

When discussing quality in education we soon find that the conceptual problems form a jungle which has to be cleared before tangible criteria can be identified and a meaningful debate about quality and its assesment can be conducted.

Both educators and laymen often use the word 'standards' when evaluating the quality of school education. The expression has certain vague connotations. In the first place, 'standards' are thought of as being almost metaphysically anchored. It is regarded as a sacrilege to change 'standards,' especially of course to lower them. It is striking to note how, at least in Europe, all steps that have been taken to broaden the opportunities for secondary and higher education have met with the objection that they would 'lower the standards.' When educators who frequently use the expression are asked to provide an operational definition of what they mean by 'standards,' they are usually at a loss. If pressed for some meaning, they might come out with the definition that 'standards' refer to minimum requirements for a pass mark that have crystallized over the years. Thus, one finds that in European secondary academic schools the failure rate in any given country and type of school has, over a long period of time, tended to be almost constant, and strikingly independent of the size of the enrollment.

Quality refers to educational *products*, not to the resources and processes from which the products emerge. Resources, financial and others, such as per-pupil expenditure, class size and teacher salaries, are in affluent countries only tenuously correlated with the quality of the products in terms, for instance, of student achievement (Passow *et al.*, 1976). The cost development (in terms of per-pupil expenditure) in, for instance, Sweden since the early 1960s is a case in point (Husén, 1979). It may well be that resources in affluent, highly industrialized, countries are available beyond the point of diminishing return in terms of student achievement. A stronger correlation between, on the one hand, resources in terms of teacher competence or class size and, on the other, student achievements has been found in developing countries (Husén *et al.*, 1978).

Quality means to what extent the *objectives* set for certain educational activities going on in schools have been achieved. There are obvious difficulties in attempts to *operationalize* these objectives. The Education Policies Commission in the United States fifty years ago came up with major sets of goals which were then broken down into sub-goals. This eventually led to demands for a 'taxonomy' of educational objectives. Such a taxonomy was developed by Benjamin Bloom (1956) and his co-workers. When the National Assessment of Educational Progress

(NAEP) was launched in the United States under the leadership of Ralph Tyler, a system of operationalizing objectives in key subject areas by drawing upon the experiences and opinions of enlightened citizens was worked out (Tyler, 1985).

Even though 'product assessment,' as a rule by measuring *cognitive* competencies, is the main approach in measuring quality, there are also attempts to use other indicators of the quality of the educative milieu or climate of a given school or school system (see, e.g., Rutter *et al.*, 1979). Examples of such indicators are absenteeism, delinquency, drug abuse, dropout, and teacher turnover.

Evidently, if we were to use student achievements, however measured, as the sole indicator of the quality of school education, we would be unduly reductionistic. The objectives of school education in all countries are also expressed in terms of character formation and personality development. The school is expected to bring about changes in the students which are not confined to the cognitive domain. It is expected to make its contributions to the development of certain attitudes and behaviors that will bring about responsible, co-operative, participating, and independent citizens with due appreciation of the national culture and with a behavior guided by moral and esthetic values.

Psychological research has since Alfred Binet in 1905 published his *échelle métrique* developed increasingly refined methods by means of which cognitive competences, be they outcomes of school learning or more 'pure' intelligence, can be measured with a reasonable validity and reliability which by far exceed impressionistic assessments. The situation is, however, far less satisfactory when it comes to measuring attitudes, values and social behavior. Even though some progress was made already back in the 1920s, the first major attempt to do so in evaluating the less tangible outcomes of schooling was ventured in the Eight-Year Study in the early 1940s by Ralph Tyler and his associates (Smith *et al.*, 1942). Further attempts, although with more limited success because of the size of the enterprise, were made by IEA both in the first mathematics study (Husén, 1967) and subsequently in the so-called Six-Subject Survey (Walker, 1976). Finally, the National Assessment of Educational Progress in the United States should be mentioned (Tyler, 1985).

Therefore, when talking about the quality of education the concern has almost invariably been about *cognitive* outcomes in terms of student achievement or sometimes the groundwork laid by secondary schools for university education. The criteria employed in assessing the quality of education are therefore cognitive ones, normally expressed as scores on standardized tests, such as the Scholastic Aptitude Test taken by almost two million students in American high schools every year or the so-called standard test in the three Rs taken by entire cohorts at certain grade levels in Swedish schools or the international tests in seven subject areas developed by IEA.

Quality Indicators

In measuring the quality of a school three kinds of indicators have been used: (1) the 'inputs,' the financial or other resources available to the school, (2) the teaching-learning process in terms of time for school learning, amount of homework and curricular provisions, and (3) the 'products' in terms of student achievement as assessed, for instance, by means of standardized tests.

For a long time quality was measured by resources (see, e.g., Mort, 1946). Some economists still use these as major quality criteria, such as teacher/pupil ratio, per-pupil expenditure, size of non-teaching support staff or library facilities. But, as pointed out above, input and process variables can only be used as proxies for product variables.

When large-scale surveys of educational outcomes, such as the Equality of Educational Opportunity Survey (Coleman *et al.*, 1966) or the IEA cross-national evaluation studies (Walker, 1976), have been conducted, it has usually been found that the resources that go into a school tend to be rather weakly related to outcomes. It has furthermore been found that only a rather small fraction of the between-school variance in terms of student achievement can be accounted for by resources, such as per-student expenditure (see Hanushek, 1981). Home background tends to account for by far the greatest part of variance both between schools and between students. This does, however, not mean that 'schooling does not make any difference' but simply that above a certain threshold of resources, where most schools in so-called developed countries are located, home background contributes more to differential outcomes than schooling. This also explains why teacher-pupil ratio within a wide margin of variation, say from fifteen to thirty-five pupils in the class, shows no measurable relationship with student achievements (see Glass, 1985).

As pointed out above, criteria of quality in education have ideally to be derived from the objectives set for a system or a sub-system of education. Some of these objectives are in the final analysis social ones which are shared by other institutions in society and not just limited to school education. Such an overriding objective is the ability to play a competent, participatory role as a citizen in a democratic society which has been made explicit in various documents prepared by authoritative bodies, such as the Educational Policies Commission in the United States.

A similar document is the national curriculum for the Swedish comprehensive school issued by the government in 1962, 1969, and 1980 respectively. An overriding objective here was to achieve better equality of educational opportunity and to promote more equality of life chances by paying more attention to students who have difficulties following the learning pace of their classmates. Adequate 'basic skills' have, not least in recent years, been strongly emphasized against a background of the fact that a great number of students after nine to eleven years leave school as functional illiterates. Finally, the common core of mandatory school education is expected to lay the ground for a useful vocational training.

These overriding objectives have in the first place to be broken down and specified in terms of sub-goals which can be achieved by setting up a hierarchy such as the one by Bloom (1956) and his associates. They can, however, only be partially operationalized and in the final analysis subjected to objective measurement.

Problems in Comparing National Systems

In studying changes of student achievements on a comparative basis one has to face two kinds of methodological problems: (1) variations *over time* in national or local systems of education, and (2) variations *between* (as a rule) *national systems*. The latter can also be studied over time, which has been the case in launching second surveys in mathematics and science by the International Association for the Evaluation of Educational Achievement. Most empirical evidence available relates to the former type of studies. The most noted and debated case is the observed changes of the Scholastic Aptitude Test (SAT) scores in the United States since the late 1960s, which gave rise to a series of analytical studies (see, e.g., Wiley and Harnischfeger, 1975). The other notable illustration also refers to the United States, namely the National Assessment of Educational Progress (NAEP) with repeated measurements over more than ten years of 9, 13, 17 year olds and adults (Tyler, 1985).

The only major source of empirical evidence, when it comes to cross-national comparisons, consists of the IEA surveys (Husén, 1967; Walker, 1976). Again it should be mentioned that the 1964 mathematics survey was repeated in 1980–81 and the 1970 science survey in 1983–84. Comparisons both within and between national systems over time are conducted by having a set of so-called bridge items which are common to the tests administered at the two occasions.

In England data are available on the reading competence of British children at different times. The interpretation of the changes, which were cited and commented upon in the Bullock report 1975 (HMSO, 1975), have been controversial among other things because of the changes in the composition in the populations compared over time.

Comparisons Over Time

In the first place one has to consider the enormous difficulties of separating and measuring the effects of the school within *the socializing and educating environment* in its totality. Over the last decade one has begun to realize the necessity of considering the overall 'ecology' (Cremin, 1976) of educative influences that in interaction determine the development of children. How do we separate in- and out-of-school conditions and experiences? Major changes have taken place in the ecology of education over the last few decades. In the highly industrialized and urbanized countries family structure has changed dramatically. The proportion of mothers with children of school age working outside the home has increased dramatically. The one-parent family is soon the typical family constellation. In some countries children are exposed to television during school age for almost the same number of hours as they are to classroom teaching. Coleman *et al.* (1982) point out in their study of the achievements of public and private school children in America that 'family withdrawal' has become an increasingly frequent phenomenon at a time when, due to increased life expectancy, child bearing and rearing takes up a relatively short time of adult life.

The difficulties of disentangling *family* from school influences were encountered in comparing private and public high schools in the United States. 'Despite extensive statistical controls on parental background, there may very well be other unmeasured factors in the selfselection into the private sector that are associated with higher achievement.' (Coleman *et al.*, 1982, p. 180)

Curricular changes, or rather changes in the syllabuses over time, as reflected in textbooks and other instructional materials, can in a significant way affect learning outcomes in certain topics. One example is the impact of the 'new' mathematics in the 1960s in several countries. This can also be assessed by comparing the importance attached to various topics by the experts on mathematics teaching. Another example is provided by the changes in competence profiles in science between 1970 and 1983. In the United States students performed better than in 1983 on items that measured independent thinking, whereas there was no change in performance on items requiring mainly recollection of factual information.

Changes in the *structure* of the respective national systems can affect distribution of achievements. Several countries have gone through major reforms of the lower secondary stage between 1964 and 1980, the interval between the first and the second international mathematics study. When the first survey was conducted, the United States' high schools, catering for almost 90 per cent of the children in the relevant age groups, had no formal parallel system of the kind that dominated in countries like Britain and the Federal Republic of Germany. But since then these two countries have gone through major changes to the extent that in Britain the majority of secondary students go to comprehensive schools. This has to be considered in interpreting changes in, for instance, science scores between 1970 and 1983.

Changes in the total *enrollment* could have occurred at a stage on which on the first occasion only a fraction of the age group entered. This has occurred in some European countries. In the debate in the United States on the declining SAT scores it has been suggested that the change might partly be due to changes in the tested population, for instance by more high school students taking the test.

The methodological problems spelled out above encountered in comparing standards over time within national systems of education also apply in conducting cross-national comparisons. There are, however, additional problems in comparing student achievements across countries. The most obvious problem is connected with differences between countries in traditions and in educational history. This is, for instance, reflected in differences between countries in terms of centralization and local autonomy when it comes to preparing curricula, providing funds, giving examinations and providing instructional materials. Thus one finds wide differences in the relative importance attached to various subjects as reflected in the number of years and hours per week of instruction. Science ranks high on the priority scale in Japan, whereas in France it traditionally has been given a lower rating than classical languages. In the IEA feasibility study a factor analysis of the correlations between test items over countries was conducted. The French-speaking countries differed markedly from the English-speaking on the science factor (Foshay, 1962).

There are important structural differences in school organization between countries, such as with regard to age of entry, age when organizational differentiation takes place by channeling some students into academic schools or tracks, and length of mandatory school attendance. The influence of these factors have been studied by means of data from the first mathematics study (Postlethwaite, 1967). Further studies of the impact of such factors have been conducted with data from the Six-Subject Survey (Walker, 1976). For instance, the 10 year olds in Sweden score in reading and science at about the same level as those in Britain who enter school almost two years earlier or those in the continental European countries and North America who enter one year earlier. Such findings have important implications for educational policy in countries where the relative advantages and disadvantages of changing the age of school entry are discussed.

In comparing student achievements in a particular subject area, such as science, one has, of course, to take into account differences between countries in curricular provisions. Systems of education, be they national or regional, differ with regard to when a subject is introduced in the curriculum, how many years the subject is taken and how many hours per week the subject is taught. These variables were in the IEA surveys subsumed under 'opportunity to learn' a given subject or part of it. In the IEA Six-Subject Survey between-country variation in opportunity to learn was measured by means of teachers' ratings.

Conclusions

This chapter has dealt with the problems of assessing the 'quality' or 'standards' of school education as distinct from the wide variety of influences of an informal or non-formal character. Since the tasks of school education in various national systems of education are performed within different social and economic settings one can, given the widely different socio-cultural conditions, hardly employ identical criteria in evaluating the quality of education. Criteria of quality refer to what extent the schools have succeeded in achieving their cognitive and non-cognitive objectives, both the immediate and remote ones. Quality can refer either to absolute or 'criterion-referenced' standards or to relative or 'norm-referenced' ones. In the first case there is a set of minimum competencies, such as functional literacy or arithmetic needed for everyday transactions. In the second case group or individual performances are related to the distribution, including the mean score, of a reference population. The International Baccalauréat examination from secondary school is an example of the former type of evaluation. The IEA surveys exemplify the latter type.

The operationalization of criteria into measures, such as tests, has to overcome methodological difficulties, most of which derive from the vast difference between measuring cognitive and non-cognitive outcomes of school education, the former being much more accessible to available measurement techniques. This means that most criteria translated into testable standards have by necessity been limited to *cognitive* outcomes in the traditional school subjects. Feasibility studies show that it is possible to devise standardized tests by means of which student competence in certain school subjects can be measured across countries. The pervasive problem, even with good instruments, is the difficulty of separating the effects of the school from those of the home or the environment at large. Several large-scale surveys have shown that between-student and between-school differences to a large extent are accounted for by students' home background.

The comparability of standards achieved in various national systems of education reflect different educational traditions expressed in deeply ingrained differences in the relative importance attached to the various school subjects and the topics included in the teaching of them. An equally important problem is the one of separating and measuring the effect of the school within the total pattern of a socializing environment. Since major changes in that pattern have taken place, comparisons over time are also confounded by non-scholastic factors. Differences between countries in curricular provisions make it difficult to devise international achievement tests which are equally valid in all countries. Even with an international 'core' test, to which national options can be added, one has to reckon with various degrees of acceptability of the items included in the test.

Structural differences, such as variations in age of school entry and length of mandatory (or voluntary) formal schooling, have to be considered as well as organizational differentiation, for instance the siphoning off of the more academically talented at a relatively early or late age.

Cross-national differences, such as these, have to be considered in making comparisons within and/or between national systems of education.

References

Becker, H. (1979) Initiating and Implementing Reforms: The Case of the Federal Republic of Germany. In: Torsten Husén (Ed.) (1979) *The Future of Formal Education: The Role of Schooling in an Industrial Society*. Symposium at the Royal Academy of Sciences. Stockholm: Almqvist and Wiksell International, pp. 61–83.

Bereday, G., W. Brickman and G. Read (1960) *The Changing Soviet School*. Cambridge, Mass.: Riverside Press.

Bestor, A. (1953) *Educational Wastelands: A Retreat from Learning in the Public Schools*. Urbana, Illinois: University of Illinois Press.

Bloom, B. S. *et al.* (1956) *Taxonomy of Educational Objectives: Cognitive Domain*. New York: David McKay.

Carroll, J. B. (1975) *The Teaching of French as a Foreign Language*. International Studies in Evaluation V. Stockholm and New York: Almqvist and Wiksell International and John Wiley and Sons (Halsted Press).

Coleman, J. S. *et al.* (1966) *Equality of Educational Opportunity*. Washington, DC: US Department of Health, Education and Welfare, Office of Education.

Coleman, J. S. *et al.* (1982) *High School Achievement: Public, Catholic and Private Schools Compared*. New York: Basic Books.

Cox, C. B. and A. E. Dyson (Eds) (1969) *Fight for Education: A Black Paper*. London: The Critical Quarterly Society.

Cox, C. B. and A. E. Dyson (Eds) (1970) *Black Paper Two: The Crisis in Education*. London: The Critical Quarterly Society.

Cremin, L. A. (1976) *Public Education*. New York: Basic Books.

Foshay, A. W. *et al.* (1962) *Educational Achievements of Thirteen-Year-Olds in Twelve Countries*. Hamburg: Unesco Institute for Education.

Glass, G. V. (1985) Class Size. In: *International Encyclopedia of Education*. Oxford: Pergamon Press.

Halls, W. D. (1985) International Baccalauréate. In: *International Encyclopedia of Education*. Oxford: Pergamon Press.

Hanushek, E. A. (1981) Throwing Money at Schools. *Journal of Policy Analysis and Management*. Vol. 1, 1981–82, pp. 19–41.

HMSO (Bullock Report) (1975) *A Language for Life. A Report of the Committee of Inquiry*. London: Her Majesty's Stationery Office.

Husén, T. (1962) *Problems of Differentiation in Swedish Compulsory Schooling*. Stockholm: Svenska Bokförlaget (Scandinavian University Books).

Husén, T. (1967) *International Study of Mathematics: A Comparison Between Twelve Countries*. I–II. New York and Stockholm: John Wiley and Sons, and Almqvist and Wiksell International.

Husén, T. *et al.* (1978) *Teacher Training and Student Achievement in Less Developed Countries*. World Bank Staff Working Paper No. 310. Washington, DC: The World Bank.

Husén, T. (1979) *The School in Question*. London: Oxford University Press.

Husén, T. (1979) Evaluating Compensatory Education. In: *Proceedings of the National Academy of Education*, Vol. 6, 1979, pp. 425–486.

Husén, T. (1983) The International Context of Educational Research. *Oxford Review of Education*, Vol. 9:1, 1983, pp. 21–29.

Husén, T. (1983) Are Standards in US Schools Really Lagging Behind Those in Other Countries? *Phi Delta Kappa*, March 1983, pp. 455–461.

Judge, H. (1984) *A Generation of Schooling. English Secondary Schools since 1944*. Oxford: Oxford University Press.

Lynd, A. (1953) *Quackery in the Public Schools*. Boston: Little, Brown and Company.

Mort, P. (1946) *Principles of School Administration*. New York: McGraw-Hill.

Passow, A. H. *et al.* (1976) *The National Case Study: An Empirical Comparative Study of Twenty-One Countries*. International Studies in Evaluation VII. Stockholm and New York: Almqvist and Wiksell International, and John Wiley and Sons (Halsted Press).

Postlethwaite, T. N. (1967) *School Organization and Student Achievement: A Study Based on Achievement in Mathematics in Twelve Countries*. Stockholm: Almqvist and Wiksell International.

Rickover, H. G. (1959) *Education and Freedom*. New York: Dutton.

Rivlin, A. M. and M. P. Timpane (1975) *Planned Variation in Education: Should We Give Up or Try Harder?* Washington, DC: Brookings Institute.

Rutter, M. *et al.* (1979) *Fifteen Thousand Hours*. Cambridge, Mass.: Harvard University Press.

Smith, E. R. and R. W. Tyler (1942) *Appraising and Recording Student Progress*. New York: Harper and Brothers.

Tyler, R. W. (1985) National Assessment of Educational Progress. In: *International Encyclopedia of Education*. Oxford, Pergamon Press.

Walker, D. (1976) *The IEA Six-Subject Survey: An Empirical Study of Education in Twenty-One Countries*. International Studies in Evaluation IX. Stockholm and New York: Almqvist and Wiksell International and John Wiley and Sons (Halsted Press).

Wiley, D. E. and Annegret Harnischfeger (1975) *Achievement Test Score Decline: Do We Need To Worry?* Chicago: Cemrel Inc.

8

Assessing Research Competencies in Education: A Cross-National Exercise

Introduction

IN THE EARLY 1980s I conducted a study of resources available for educational research in the less developed regions of the world. Leading research institutions were identified by obtaining nominations from a large number of people, most of them working in multilateral aid agencies. By means of interviews and mail questionnaires the resources of these institutions in staff and financing were described and the quality of their research output assessed on the basis of the reputation it had in the international community of scholars in the field. Subsequently, I was invited to serve on a task force of three members who were asked to evaluate the 'impact' on education of the Ontario Institute of Education in Toronto, Canada.

The present chapter draws upon the experiences from these two exercises, particularly the first one. It is an attempt to identify the criteria that could be used in assessing the 'quality,' 'productivity,' and 'impact' of research institutions.

It has often been emphasized that in Third World countries one should aim to build up indigenous research capabilities. But such competencies have to be available at the *institutional* level. It usually does not suffice that a single scholar, for instance, a university professor, possesses certain expertise in an area which coincides with the fields of concern of the aid agency. If his or her competence is going to be brought to bear in, for instance, conducting evaluation or tracer studies, it must be available in an institutional context with a supporting staff for data collection, data processing, and statistical analyses. Thus, research capabilities have to be viewed and assessed in terms of institutional resources which are only partly constituted by individual competencies and expertise. Key components of institutional capacity consist of a competent, professional staff with adequate training, guaranteed continuity and adequate funding, and which takes a programmatic approach in its research.

What kind of capabilities, then, are needed for an institution that is conducting either project-related research or is responsible for data collection in connection with, for instance, comprehensive surveys? Since such projects tend to be data-intensive, the more tangible competencies are those related to collection, processing, and statistical analysis of data. It is not enough, however, for certain individuals to master such skills. Any empirical research endeavor, even the most modest one, has to be carried out with a minimum of theoretical sophistication and an ability to manage and administer projects with big data sets. Studies conducted at national level with large-scale data collection, such as testing big samples of students or gathering statistics about the flow of students through the system, require such competencies.

The Importance of Using Indigenous Research Competence

The objective of using regional and/or local competencies in educational research is part of the wider goal of promoting development at large. There are several good reasons for assisting national research institutions to study educational problems related to their own country. At least two important reasons for promoting the build-up of such competence can be given. In the first place, familiarity with the particular social and cultural reality of a country is an indisputable practical advantage, particularly in data collection. Second, there is a strong need for trained individuals who are not only equipped to collect reliable data, but whose familiarity with the cultural, linguistic and social environment facilitates a proper interpretation of these data.

Even if it ought to be recognized that scientific research by its very nature both conceptually and methodologically is international, its paradigms and methods—this applies particularly in the social sciences—are not independent of the prevailing cultural and social values in a particular society. Research techniques employed in education in Europe and North America are part and parcel of an intellectual development that has become institutionalized over a period of less than one hundred years. Empirical methods in educational studies began to be used in Germany, England, and the United States at the turn of the century in studying child development and in measuring cognitive ability by means of standardized tests. Much of this was a by-product of an experimental psychology born in the late nineteenth century. Survey techniques, which now play such an important role in the social sciences, date back to the Second World War when they began to be used in assessing attitudes and the morale among American soldiers and the effects of strategic bombing.

After the War, the Survey Research Center at the University of Michigan launched a large-scale research program which entailed studying the relationship between productivity on the one hand and employee morale and leadership styles on the other. Those and other research techniques became standard ingredients of handbooks on social research and were taught to students at American and European universities in the 1950s.

The techniques employed in the social sciences were, however, developed in societies with a high level of technology and all that goes with it in terms of a supportive infrastructure of technicians and clerical competence. This has to be kept in mind when it comes to attempts to transfer sophisticated social science methodology to societies which, to a considerable extent, are still at the subsistence economy level.

Since the early 1970s it has been part of the policy of the World Bank to involve regional and/or local research institutions in the implementation of components of the educational programs and when competence in handling certain techniques is required. Such a component is evaluation which requires survey methodology and what goes with it in terms of sampling, achievement testing, and statistical analysis. So-called tracer studies and investigations into the internal efficiency of institutions, such as universities, could also be mentioned. These and other investigations, having been conducted once as a learning experience, take on the character of routine procedures, when they are repeated and cease to carry the element of innovation or creativity that is the hallmark of research. But even in employing certain routine procedures, for instance, in connection with data collection for evaluation, these data are, in the first place, related to the social and cultural reality of the home country. Second, they can be used as a base for new investigations, for instance, in followup studies of graduates or conducting analyses of how educational attainments are related to social background.

Again, it should be recognized that research methodologies are inherently international as long as they are employed with the aim of arriving at more universally valid knowledge. There is, for instance, basically no Tanzanian or Peruvian survey methodology. But at the same time it should be recognized that these 'international' techniques have to be considerably modified in order to work better under particular national and/or local conditions. Thus, the sampling procedures used in evaluating educational programs depend very much on the nature and quality of national statistics. The communication system of a country very much determines what kind of survey strategy that can be employed in conducting and monitoring national evaluation studies.

It should be recognized that in both Europe and North America it was not until the mid-1960s that *educational* research with an empirical research strategy began to become institutionalized and equipped with resources which enabled it to begin developing a knowledge base for educational change and improvement. In assessing research capabilities in developing countries and in considering what could eventually be done in building research competencies at the institutional level in these countries, the *short history* of significant research in the field of education in Europe and North America should be kept in mind. The short history of graduate programs in education on both sides of the Atlantic is another important part of the background.

Hard-core, discipline-oriented graduate training of young people heading for research careers for a long time took place outside the departments or institutes of education. These were mainly preoccupied with providing undergraduates with the pedagogical training and practice teaching they needed for their teaching role. Students in colleges of education or education departments who proceeded to graduate degrees were often teachers who wanted to qualify for promotion, many of them on a part-time basis after a number of years of teaching experience. They often opted for research tasks in the pedagogical realm of a rather trivial and 'safe' nature with routine data collection and without complicated theoretical ramifications. This was one reason why research conducted in colleges of education was often looked down upon by scholars in other departments.

The change came in the 1950s, when leading schools of education systematically began to recruit top social scientists from other departments, such as psychology, sociology, economics, anthropology, and political science. The result was an impressive upgrading of educational research at such universities. The most glaring examples are the University of Chicago and Stanford University. But there are other places, such as Teachers College, Columbia, and London Institute of Education, where the availability of scholars from a wide range of disciplines has provided important cross-fertilization. Comparative education emerged from this as an area of study and as a separate discipline and was pivotal in studies and graduate programs in development education at places like Chicago and Pittsburgh. The Ontario Institute for Education was put in charge of the graduate program for the University of Toronto, whose college of education with a lot of professors was left with undergraduate teaching and meagre resources for research (Gage *et al.*, 1980).

Competencies Considered

'Educational research' has in this particular case been defined as social science research 'utilized' in dealing with educational problems. Education constitutes a vast field of practice and application but does not in itself constitute a scientific discipline.

Scientific disciplines relevant to educational problems fall into two broad categories: those with philosophical and historical and those with instrumental and empirical bearings. History of education and philosophy of education belong to the first category. Educational sociology, educational psychology, economics of education, educational statistics (with demography), and educational anthropology belong to the second. Comparative education cuts across the two categories of disciplines.

In continental Europe educational studies were, until the 1950s, dominated by the philosophical and historical approach, whereas in North America, given the prevailing pragmatic research paradigm, the empirical approach became predominant several decades earlier. Educational psychology with research on learning, testing, and individual differences dominated in the colleges and graduate schools of education. Until recently educational research on both sides of the Atlantic was almost entirely preoccupied with classroom pedagogy (didactics). The expectation was that by means of improved methods of studying the learning-teaching process it would be possible to arrive at generalizations about factors conducive to effective teaching and to devise improved methods of instruction. The latest, and perhaps final, big drive in that direction occurred under the auspices of the R&D movement in the United States (Keppel, 1966) financed by the Office of Education under the provisions of the Elementary and Secondary Education Act which made large funds available for the establishment of R&D centers at some American universities.

A more interdisciplinary approach in educational research began, as mentioned above, to be taken in the 1950s and 1960s when some leading universities introduced a deliberate policy of recruiting professors from departments of sociology, economics and anthropology, and giving joint appointments at these departments as well as the department of education.

Criteria in Identifying Institutions

The primary unit of analysis in a study of resources in research is, as pointed out above, the *institution* and not the individual researcher. The capability to conduct the kind of research considered here is, of course, within each particular institution dependent on individual researchers responsible for ongoing studies as principal investigators and/or project leaders. However, in order to be able to successfully complete projects which require massive data collection, certain institutional resources would have to be brought to bear, such as competent assistants and data processing facilities.

Furthermore, given the kind of problems encountered in many projects conducted within the framework of foreign aid, one should focus particularly on competencies needed in sample survey research (including techniques of conducting representative sampling in large systems of education), evaluation techniques, studies of 'productivity' of systems, studies of cultural and social values related to education, and studies of internal efficiency of institutions and systems.

The following, more specific criteria of competence can be employed:
—major thrusts of research programs as reflected in institutional publications;
—academic level of competence as evidenced by degrees of senior researchers, university affiliation, and graduate programs;
—relations with the scholarly community (e.g., citations in the International Social Science Citation Index);
—methodological sophistication;
—size of research budget;
—relations with national and international agencies working in development education.

Assessment of 'Productivity' and Quality of Research

In-depth study of research units is a task for sociology of science. So far, few major studies have been conducted on research institutes and/or units as separate entities. Most studies refer to organizational effectiveness in general. A major attempt to investigate R&D effectiveness has been conducted by Andrews *et al.* (1979) who under UNESCO auspices, in a project called 'The International Study on the Organization and Performance of Research Units,' studied some 1,200 research units with about 11,000 participants in six European countries. The main objective of the investigation was to develop a methodology for assessing the organizational effectiveness by inquiring into the managerial environment and the organizational settings of these units. The study was a clearcut social science empirical survey, including hypothesis formulation, construction of measuring instruments, standardized collection of data from large groups, and subsequent (in this case multivariate) analyses of data. The ultimate purpose was to develop indicators that could be used to assess the productivity and quality of research *units*, not primarily the individual researchers within these units.

Organizational and environmental inputs into the units that were hypothesized to influence their performance-effectiveness were identified and assessed by means of questionnaires administered to five types of respondents: (1) heads of the units; (2) academic staff; (3) technical support staff; (4) unit administrators; and (5) external evaluators. An average of about three external evaluators conveyed their opinion about the units. It should be mentioned that only 6 per cent of the units belonged to the social sciences; the overwhelming number of them came from the 'hard' sciences, particularly the natural sciences and technology.

One could object that assessments based to a large extent on ratings and responses from the units themselves easily lead to biased results, and

Andrews in a special chapter (*op. cit.* p. 405 *et seq.*) tries to estimate the so-called construct validity of the assessment variables as well as their error components. In his estimation 'slightly more than half the total variance of a typical composite performance measure is valid variance.' (p. 418) Ratings by the heads of the units as well as the staff scientists turned out to be more valid than expected and the external evaluations were 'rather low in validity and heavily saturated with bias/halo effects.' (p. 417)

Before presenting the measures employed in the Andrews *et al.* (1979) study, I shall refer to another attempt to assess the performance of a research unit, namely the studies conducted by a task force established in 1978 by the Board of Governors of the Ontario Institute for Studies in Education (Gage, Husén and Singleton, 1980). The overall purpose of setting up the task force was to assess the 'impact' of the Institute's research and development activities as well as its field work. The types of information collected included the following:

—questionnaires on impact completed by Ontario participants (in most cases teachers and school administrators) in the Institute's projects, workshops and conferences;
—questionnaires on impact completed by administrators and selected schools and board staff in every educational jurisdiction in Ontario;
—questionnaires on impact completed by Institute faculty;
—briefs or other presentations from professional associations in the province;
—information on the press coverage of the Institute;
—lists of major publications of the Institute;
—collections (with content analysis) of reviews of major Institute publications;
—analyses of citations of Institute publications and other information indicating the activity of Institute faculty and staff in scholarly and research publications;
—information on the first appointment of the Institute's doctoral graduates;
—information on the participation of Institute faculty in professional meetings, such as those of the American Educational Research Association;
—perceptions of the impact of the Institute held by selected members of the Legislative Assembly; and
—perceptions of the impact of the Institute held by selected officials of the Ontario Ministry of Education.

Most of this information lent itself to quantification. The information obtained by questionnaires and by interviews were, at best, accurate reflections of how the respondents perceived the Institute which, of course, is of great value in itself, since the groups approached were central parts of the constituency the Institute was serving. However, since such measures can only provide a picture of how well the constituencies *perceived* the Institute serving *them*, they obviously cannot be used to assess the scholarly quality of its work. Measures which have proved to be useful for this other purpose are citations in the Social Science Citation Index. Additional data on citations were obtained from an article in the Canadian Journal of Education which presented a study on the quantity and impact of scholarly journal publications of Canadian faculties of education. In this article a comparison was made between Canadian educational research institutions with regard to productivity. A content analysis of reviews of the major publications as well as staff participation in international congresses and conferences as compared to other research institutions in North America provided additional measures of scholarly quality.

Given the extensive nature of both the Andrews *et al.* (1979) study and my own review of educational research competencies in some Third World regions, one should not expect too much in terms of in-depth analysis. Even if the institutes in my case were nominated as the leading ones in their respective parts of the Third World, one should keep in mind that the nominators could have overlooked or overrated the importance of certain institutions and that the directors of the institutions who responded to our questionnaire might have given a biassed picture.

Andrews *et al.* (1979) distinguished between four types of research organizations:

(1) Academic organizations (in most cases accommodated in a university or a college).

(2) National research organizations, for instance, academies of science, or national bureaux of research.

(3) Co-operative research organizations which serve a given sector of production in industry, in public services or a single industrial enterprise.

(4) Contract research institutes which largely operate on contract or 'soft' money.

From fifty-six questionnaire variables eleven composite measures were derived. Three of the eleven were based on information on sheer quantity, such as published written outputs, patents and prototypes, and reports. The seven measures of quality were based on ratings by: (1) unit head, (2) staff scientists, and (3) external evaluators. The seven aspects of qualitative performance were:

(1) General contribution by the unit to science.

(2) Recognition from outside, such as international reputation and requests for its publications.

(3) Social effectiveness as assessed by the social value of its work.

(4) Training effectiveness.

(5) Administrative effectiveness by meeting schedules staying within budget.

(6) R&D effectiveness (productiveness, innovativeness).

(7) Application effectiveness.

Evidently, these measures were correlated with each other. They were also of highly different value as measures of quality.

The findings from the Andrews *et al.* (1979) survey shall not be discussed here, since the main interest is in the *measures* of quality and how they can be derived. Tentative results indicate, not surprisingly, that factors that account for group effectiveness in general also apply to research units, such as communication between researchers and the morale and motivation that has been achieved not least by actions of the leader of the unit. A consistent finding worth mentioning is the *absence of any significant relationship between indicators of economic and physical resources and the effectiveness of the research units*. The quality of the unit head and the satisfaction of the unit members *vis-à-vis* the quality and sufficiency of its human resources appeared to be much more important than the financial resources.

These findings have important implications for attempts to evaluate research units by means of conventional cost-benefit analyses. The unpredictability of human creativity easily makes such analyses inadequate, since there is not a nomothetic relationship between resources and output in terms of high-quality research findings. In scientific research, breakthroughs often occur in an entirely unforeseen way.

Thus, in attempting to assess the quality of a research institution, much more importance should be attached to the scholarly qualifications of its staff, particularly the ones of its head, and to the quality of research output (as assessed by the international community of scholars) than to the actual financial and staff resources available. One cannot avoid noticing how certain institutions in, for instance, Latin America have been able to acquire enormous staffs (sometimes on paper only) without having a corresponding impact on the scholarly world.

Overall Assessment of Research Competencies in Third World Countries

For each of four areas, Latin America, Asia, Africa, and the Arab regions, the research capabilities in leading institutions were assessed and lacunae of competencies identified. Some generalizations, apart from the obvious ones, are ventured.

(1) The study focussed on research in education in developing countries institutionalized at universities or ministries of education. In each region I have tried to identify what could be called centers of excellence. They are few and stand out among many mediocre and weak

institutions. Most Third World countries presently do not possess professional research competence and supporting facilities that would enable them to conduct research associated with major programs in education. In Africa as a whole, one can identify three or four institutions which could be drawn upon; in Asia and Latin America there are a few more.

(2) Empirical research in education has, even in Europe and North America, a rather short history. Competencies in conducting relevant research by means of, for instance, survey techniques are very unequally distributed. The unequal distribution of research capabilities is, of course, closely related to the availability of adequately trained professional staff. Since, as indicated above, modern empirically-oriented educational research developed rather recently in Europe and North America, graduate studies in the field by students from developing countries have almost exclusively been taken overseas. I have noted that in the centers of excellence identified in the developing countries most leading researchers have graduated from leading American or European universities. Many of them are products of the few centers which provide graduate programs in development education, such as SIDEC at Stanford University, the Comparative Education Center at the University of Chicago, and the London Institute of Education.

(3) It is impossible to generalize about any 'major thrusts' in ongoing research. Institutions founded with an explicitly policy-oriented mission to provide a knowledge base for major educational changes at the national level, such as the Office of Educational and Cultural Research and Development (BP 3K) in Indonesia, the Centro de Investigaciones y Servicios Educativos (CISE) in Mexico or the Centro Multinacional de Investigación Educativa (CEMIE) in Costa Rica, the entire research program becomes geared to wide-scale surveys, testing programs, etc. But in research units operating within the framework of a traditional university department, the research picture tends to become as diversified as are the interests of the individual researchers.

In many places, where educational research is conducted, the picture is dominated by what for a long time, particularly in the education departments in the United States, was regarded as central and genuinely educational, namely inquiries into methods of instruction, that is to say, pedagogy.

(4) Two types of capabilities are conspicuously lacking in many places: competence to conduct surveys and to process, analyze, and adequately store large sets of data collected in comprehensive surveys. These have for practical and financial reasons in most cases tended to be sample surveys. This requires both competence in data processing, statistical analysis and access to reliable administrative statistical information from central agencies. Furthermore, since evaluation surveys require large-scale testing programs, there is a need for researchers with a basic training in tests

and measurements who are able to develop and try out instruments adequate not only for a particular type of survey but for a particular country and/or culture as well.

The techniques used to handle, i.e., to process and analyze, large sets of data have developed concomitantly with the survey methods and the use of computers in data processing and statistical analysis. Capabilities in this field have, in many developing countries, been established in a remarkably short period of time. It seems to take less time to develop that part of the research infrastructure which consists of skills needed to handle data processing instruments than to establish competencies to plan and design major empirical studies and carry out statistical analyses of the data collected.

(5) Since most senior professional staff in educational research institutions in developing countries have been trained at overseas universities, they have not only been socialized into the prevailing research paradigms but also been used to dealing with educational problems as they present themselves in the host countries. This often makes them blind to the appearance of these problems in their own countries. They have often had to collect data for their theses in the host country, which makes them further neglect problems in their home countries. For example, studies of how home background relates to school achievements have, in developing countries, to be conceived within a framework of background variables different from those usually included in industrial societies.

References

Andrews, F. M. *et al.* (1979) *Scientific Productivity: The Effectiveness of Research in Six Countries.* Cambridge, England: Cambridge University Press.

Council of Europe (1974) *Politique de Recherche Educationelle dans les Pays Européennes.* Strasbourg: Council of Europe.

Gage, N. L., T. Husén and J. Singleton (1980) *Report of the Task Force on the Impact of the Research, Development and Field Activities of the Ontario Institute for Studies in Education.* Toronto, Ontario: OISE.

Husén, T. (1977) 'Pupils, Teachers and Schools in Botswana: A National Evaluation Survey of Primary and Secondary Education'. In: *Education for Kagisano.* Vol. 2: Annexes.

Husén, T., L. Saha and R. Noonan (1978) *Teacher Training and Student Achievement in Less Developed Countries.* Washington, DC: World Bank Staff Working Paper No. 310.

Husén, T. and M. Kogan, Eds. (1984) *Educational Research and Policy: How Do They Relate?* Oxford: Pergamon Press.

Karabel, J. and A. H. Halsey (1977) *Power and Ideology in Education.* Edited with Introduction by Jerome Karabel and A. H. Halsey. London: Oxford University Press.

Keppel, F. (1966) *The Necessary Revolution in American Education.* New York: Harper and Row.

Myers, R. G. (1981) *Connecting Worlds: A Survey of Developments in Educational Research.* Ottawa, Ontario.

Niessen, M. and J. Peschar, Eds. (1982) *Comparative Research in Education: Overview, Strategy and Applications in Eastern and Western Europe.* London: Pergamon Press.

Research Strengths of Universities in the Developing Countries of the Commonwealth. London: The Association of Commonwealth Universities.

III

Reform

Introduction

EDUCATIONAL REFORMS usually take place within the framework of national systems of education, rather independently of the degree of central steering. Reforms have to do with changes in structures of the systems and contents of their curricula (including methods of teaching) which aim to achieve certain overriding objectives, such as more equality of provision or higher quality as reflected in better work performances of its citizens. In this section two cases are taken up: Spain and Britain. The first is used to illustrate what is advanced as basic 'strategy rules' for reforms.

Twenty-five years ago, hopes were high about what educational technology, such as television, teaching machines and programmed teaching could do in order to help us cope with the enrollment explosion, and to improve classroom learning. We have gradually begun to realize that technology cannot substitute teachers in performing what is at the center of the educative tasks, but can supplement the teachers, not least when it comes to practicing of skills. The first chapter in this section attempts to take stock of the experiences gained.

As pointed out earlier in this book, international co-operation in education promoted by organizations such as UNESCO and OECD as well as

99

by multinational involvement in assisting developing countries in building up their systems of education, has contributed to a remarkable widening of the perspective within which educational problems are conceived.

There are fundamental problems pertaining to educational objectives which transcend national boundaries and break up old provincial limitations. Two such problems are dealt with in this section, the first has to do with the need for intellectual coherence in a complex and fragmented world. It is argued that the study of history can contribute to such coherence. The other is related to the time-honored problem of what constitutes general education and how to resolve the dilemma of integrated knowledge in an era of highly specialized disciplines and sub-disciplines. The concept of 'global learning' is used to convey the idea of integrated learning both in terms of problems which concern the entire world and in terms of studying these problems in a more integrated, that is to say interdisciplinary, way.

Notes

[1]Paper presented at the Fundación Santillana, Conference on *La educación ante las innovaciones científicas y tecnologicas*, December 1987. Published by Fundación Santillana, Madrid in 1988.
[2]Paper prepared in English and published in translation as 'Reglas estratégicas para reforma educativa' in *Revista de ciències de l'educación*, Serie II, Vol. I, Universitad de Barcelona, 1987 and later in *Interchange*, Vol. 19, No. 3–4, 1988.
[3]Published in *Oxford Review of Education*, Vol. 14, No. 3, 363–369, 1988.
[4]Paper given at the School of Education, University of California 1984.
[5]An adaptation of a paper prepared for the United Nations University in 1986.

9

Enrollment Explosion: Can the New Technologies Offer a Solution?

Introduction

SCIENCE AND its translation into technology has made two major impacts on modern society. First, it has in many respects reshaped our daily life. It has given us new ways of maintaining our health, not least by new marvelous drugs. It has made home work much easier and more comfortable by all kinds of labor-saving devices and machines. It has facilitated communications and transportation. In working life it has saved us quite a lot of toil and drudgery. But on a global scale it has also had an impact on our ecology with air and water pollution, acid rain, and destruction of the ozone layer. Chernobyl gave us a lesson in what nuclear plant disasters can mean for entire regions of the world. The side-effects of technology have, however, only during the last few decades become a major concern. When James B. Conant (1947), whose book *On Understanding Science* I shall come back to later, prepared the lectures which were published in the book, he had only one concern, but a major one, about science: namely the atom bomb that had been used at the end of the War a year before. He quoted Emerson: 'With every influx of light comes new danger.' But nowhere in his book was any reference made to the environmental impact of technology, nor to the disaffection with science and technology that has become so widespread among young people since the late 1960s.

Second, modern science, not least microelectronics, has been instrumental in giving us devices like radio, television and, recently, computers which have entered, not to say invaded, the field of education. 'Educational technology' at the end of the 1960s became a household word. The new devices were expected to facilitate the learning process, to make teaching much more expedient, and even substitute teachers. I know of a university that in the 1960s was designed on the premise that

101

much of the instruction would be taken care of by internal television, teaching machines and language laboratories. This was in the 'golden sixties,' when the expectations of what educational technology would be able to achieve were running high. As I shall spell out later, we have since then become more realistic.

In this chapter I should like to focus mainly on the impact of science and technology as an instrument of making instruction in schools or instruction in general more efficient. But before that I cannot resist the temptation to express my views about the place of science in modern, democratic society in educating an enlightened citizenry. This is, I submit, something different from teaching the elements of science to school children. What I have in mind here is the need to widen the perspective and to make citizens aware of the social and ecological impact of science and technology. In dealing with his problem I shall take James B. Conant as my starting point.

In 1947 Conant, then President of Harvard University, who during the Second World War had played a leading role in advisory bodies on research appointed by the Federal Government in the United States, and had followed the process of research and development leading up to the atomic bomb, was invited to give the Terry Lectures at Yale University. They were the same year published under the title *On Understanding Science*. Conant, an outstanding scholar and researcher in chemistry (see his autobiography *My Several Lives*, New York: Harper and Row, 1970) had as a new university president taken a keen interest in educational problems, an interest he was to pursue further during a later stage of his life with his studies of the American high school and its problems. He had taken the initiative to establish a Graduate School of Education at Harvard and had been instrumental in setting up what later became the Educational Testing Service in Princeton, an organization which promoted his idea that ability and merit rather than family background should determine the recruitment of students to top universities like Harvard.

Given the nature of the political process in modern democracy, a widespread understanding of science is a necessary ingredient of the general education given to the common voter and citizen. Such an understanding is a prerequisite for science to be assimilated into the secular culture of our 'age of machines and experts.' To achieve such a goal is, of course, a huge pedagogic task both in school and adult education. Because of the fact the applications of science play so important a part in our daily lives, matters of policy are profoundly influenced by highly technical scientific considerations. Perhaps the most illuminating example of this is the public debate about security problems related to nuclear energy plants.

Conant quotes Karl Pearson's classical book *The Grammar of Science*, which was published in 1892, almost one hundred years ago with the optimistic message that the scientific method with its 'impartial and rational enquiries' would provide an 'education specially fitted to promote sound citizenship' (p. 6). Conant takes issue with Pearson's view that the study of science *per se* is the best education and finds it 'a very dubious . . . hypothesis at best.' But he thinks that there is after all something in it. He refers to this as 'understanding science,' which in essence is to be conceived of as a special frame of mind. He defines it as a 'feel' for 'the strategy and tactics of science,' which is not the same thing as being well-informed about the factual state of the art in science. The frame of mind called 'understanding' can be brought about by 'retracing the steps by which certain results have been produced.' In a way, a study of the history of science can help us to get that understanding. In two chapters of his book, Conant presents a series of historical cases, such as the water pump, Boyle's law experiment, and Volta's electric battery. He proposes that such cases could be included in a course at undergraduate level, a course that would not aim at laying the foundations of knowledge but to give the 'feels.'

In the Preface to his book Conant, after having talked about walking 'along the tightrope of atomic age,' points out that science is 'neither a benign nor malignant activity of man.' Science is a process of 'unveiling many things, all of which have their "cracks." Whether we have the courage to face the most recent evidence (i.e., the nuclear energy) of the "fatal law" and intelligence enough to proceed with the next stage in the development of our civilization will in part depend on *education* (my italics). This fact is justification enough to spend the rest of our lives trying to improve education and of "perpetuating learning to posterity."'

Cross-National Surveys of Science: Contributions by IEA

The IEA has conducted two major cross-national surveys of science education, one in 1970 and the other one in 1984. The first (Comber and Keeves, 1973) comprised nineteen countries, all but three industrial ones. The second comprised twenty-five, of which ten were developing countries. In the first survey a Test On Understanding Science (TOUS) was administered. The test drew heavily on one originally developed by Cooley and Klopfer (1961). TOUS is measuring the understanding of the nature and methodology of science, what Conant refers to as the 'strategy and tactics of science' as distinct from the content or particular items of knowledge.

A separate scale in the first survey measured what was referred to as 'Science in the World.' The scale measured to what extent science 'is perceived as being detrimental and restrictive to thinking' (Comber and Keeves, p. 109). High scores indicate that science is seen as beneficial to mankind. The mean scores for some countries and the 14 and 18 year old populations respectively have been presented in Table 1. The scales have a standardized mean of zero for all the participating countries. Positive scores indicate better understanding and less concern of science respectively.

TABLE 1

Mean Scores on the Test on Understanding Science (TOUS) and Science in the World for Populations II and IV (14 and 18 year olds). The standardized mean score is 0.

Country	TOUS Populations		Science in the world Populations	
	II	IV	II	IV
Australia	0.55	0.70	0.07	0.05
Belgium (French)	−1.48	−0.48	−0.21	−0.20
England	0.07	0.26	−0.16	−0.08
France	—	−0.55	—	−0.24
Hungary	−0.29	−0.55	0.99	0.90
Japan	0.42	—	−0.08	—
Sweden	−0.04	−0.29	−0.20	−0.38
USA	0.68	−0.10	0.39	0.20
Spread (SD)	2.68	2.63	3.56	3.79

Source: Comber and Keeves, 1973.

It is, indeed, difficult to interpret the cross-national differences shown in the Table. French-speaking countries show a lower level of understanding the nature of science than Anglo-Saxon ones and Japan. French-speaking countries also take a more negative view on science in the world, whereas Hungary, with its outstanding record in science, and the United States students take a more positive stance.

In the second international science study the national curricula were structured in fifty-seven content areas under four major disciplinary headings: earth science, biology, chemistry and physics. In addition there were 'cross-disciplinary' areas, such as environmental science and health science. The objectives of science education fell under processes, applications, manual skills, attitudes and orientations. For each national system a profile could be drawn up with regard to content emphasis rated by all the participating teachers.

Achievements consistently show striking sex differences in both science surveys. Data in the first survey were subjected to a detailed analysis by Kelly (1978). The same pattern of differences was found both across countries and across social strata within countries. This did not support the hypothesis that sex differences are accounted for mainly by cultural and social factors. The same pattern emerged in countries with educational systems having quite a different cultural and historical background. Briefly, the differences were rather small at the 10 year old level but increased steadily over the 14 to the 18 year old level. Differences were relatively small in biology, moderate in chemistry and large in physics. Data from the second international science study are available for six items in nine countries (Rosier, 1987). In the six science items (which were included also in the first international science study) sex differences were on average 10 per cent ranging from 7 to 14 per cent. It still remains to be investigated in more depth to what extent such differences are 'deep-seated,' or even inherited, or whether they are part of a socio-cultural pattern that cuts across many different countries and cultures in various parts of the world, both in industrial and in non-industrial societies.

Educational Impact of Technology

Modern, highly technological and information-based society has in many respects had a strong impact on the educational systems. Life-long or continuing education has become a pervasive feature of what often is referred to as the post-industrial society. We need to step back and try to get a better perspective before we can discuss what effects these changes have on society, particularly on the formal school system. Let me draw up three main perspectives.

(1) Knowledge, as spelled out by Daniel Bell in his book *The Coming of Post-Industrial Society* (1973), is increasingly becoming the power base for individuals and groups of individuals. It is substituting inherited wealth, and to a large extent social background, as a springboard for individual career and status. Industrialization once saw a new powerful class of capitalists, owners of the new means of production, rising to power and replacing the feudal landowners. But in a society on the verge of the post-industrial stage, where manufacturing industry is relegated to second-order importance, the possession of knowledge and acquired competence is replacing the ownership of physical and monetary capital as a basis of power. Highly trained top executives tend to have more to say in running the big companies than the stock owners. Countries in the highly techno-logical world are—irrespective of their political orders, socialist or market capitalist—moving headlong into a meritocratic stage where education becomes the democratic substitute for family background. The amount of formal education and acquired special competence has become the first criterion of selection and promotion on the job market. I shall not dwell on the meritocratic syndrome here, since I have done so at some length in my book *Talent, Equality and Meritocracy* (1974).

(2) Science has over the last few decades emerged as a key subject area in school education. Science teaching has increasingly been required to respond to the changing nature of society as well as the needs of national development. One only needs to mention microelectronics and biotech-nology in order to hint at new fields which in recent years have enor-

mously expanded. Given the increased importance of science for modern technology, which in its turn is spurred by increased international competition for markets and military supremacy, competent teaching of science has become a major problem. This has been further aggravated by two circumstances. First, most highly technological societies have difficulty in recruiting competent science teachers because of the competition with private and public enterprises in technology. Second, the disaffection with science among young people, who tend to feel that the adverse effects of technology on, for instance, the environment and the military use of it, can be blamed on science.

(3) The impact of modern technology on education has, as far as educators are concerned, been in schools where it has been perceived to have great potential for classroom instruction (Skinner, 1954). New devices have emerged on the pedagogical scene since the middle of this century as a means of making instruction more efficient by facilitating student learning, or by replacing—at least partially—the teacher.

Three 'Waves' of Educational Technology

We have since the early 1950s witnessed three major 'waves' of educational technology, each of them carried by the same enthusiasm, not to say euphoria, about the potential of the new devices. They have all been expected to reshape school education almost entirely. The history, at least of the first two waves, could be written under the adequate heading 'The rise and fall of educational technology.' Whether this applies to the last one, the one of the computers, remains to be seen, because we are now in the midst of the third wave.

First, television in education was launched, as was radio instruction a couple of decades earlier, with the hope that it would, apart from facilitating teaching-learning in general, save the teacher's time. Well structured teaching material prepared by the most outstanding pedagogues in the subject area could be televised to all children who were thereby exposed to outstanding instead of mediocre teaching. A striking illustration of this is a Ford Foundation supported project in the United States around 1960, when an airplane circled a number of Middle West states televising science material to a large number of classrooms.

Attempts were made at an early stage to evaluate the effect of educational television in terms of student competence. A review by Siegel and Siegel involving hundreds of evaluative studies, including those with experiment-control group design, by and large came to the conclusion that educational television did not add significantly to student competence.

One realized that one important shortcoming common to radio, film and television was that they were restricted to one-way communication.

Even a teacher who most of the time indulges in 'frontal instruction,' i.e., turning to the whole class, has at least some two-way communication with his or her students.

The arrival of programmed material and teaching machines claimed to solve that problem. The way the teaching material was presented in programmed teaching, i.e., by machines, seemed to establish two-way communication, because depending upon his response the student was exposed to the next step in the programmed material. At the basis of the technique was the psychological principle of operant conditioning, which was translated into a technology via the programming and the presentation by the machine. Thus, in a way, this new technology made two-way, although rigid, communication possible and was seen as a step forward in comparison with educational television. But strangely enough programmed learning and teaching machines that were so prominently *en vogue* in the early 1960s soon did not seem to be the grand solution to more effective teaching. They had almost entirely faded away by the early 1970s.

Already in the 1960s computer-assisted instruction (CAI) was launched as a more flexible *interactive* device than both television and the Skinnerian teaching machines. I remember visiting with Professor Patrick Suppes of Stanford University a school in East Palo Alto where children from that slum area were practicing reading and arithmetic by computer. The terminals at the school were connected with the Stanford University Computer Center. CAI could patently provide an enormous amount of practice but was by no means cost-effective. It would probably have been a much better economy to let teachers provide individualized practice sessions!

But in the 1980s we have now entered the stage where minicomputers are invading the schools and in some instances are available in every classroom. This has, of course, made the use of computer in school instruction much cheaper and much easier to administer.

The minicomputers can be used for instructional purposes once the suitable 'software,' i.e., programmed material, is available. There is, however, an additional reason for making students familiar with computers, namely their growing role in society at large, not least in working life. Home computers are almost commonplace. Banking and retail business in many countries have already become computerized. In school education we are now putting stronger emphasis on what is referred to as 'computer literacy' than on the facilitation of classroom instruction with assistance of the computer. The problem met in using computers in school instruction is the need for adequate software, properly programmed material, where quite a lot of work has to be done by the actual classroom teacher who cannot rely on what has been done centrally. The software, however, has by no means kept pace with the development of hardware which has turned out to be an impediment in using computers for teaching-learning purposes.

In recent years microcomputers and terminals linked to computer centers have made quite a lot of headway. Are they likely to make an impact over the next couple of decades? According to figures from the National Center for Educational Statistics in Washington, DC, there were already in 1982 some 100,000 microcomputers and 26,000 terminals in the 82,000 American schools. About one third had at least one computer, and quite a few had several.

There is one feature of the technology offered by the computers which makes it by far superior to both television and teaching-machine mediated instruction of the 1960s. It can provide *two-way communication*. This feature carries the following possibilities:

(1) Storing and retrieving of the detailed data about each individual student enables the school and its teachers to monitor the progress of students and groups of students without any extra expenditures of time and money.

(2) Computers provide more flexible arrangements for individualized instruction than the early teaching-machine facilities.

(3) Computers require quite a lot of activity on the part of the student right from the beginning, whereas he usually has no part at all in the preparation of TV programs. He can also experience the excitement of interacting with the computer.

(4) Computer-assisted instruction of this type is much cheaper than previous technologies, but—still—the software problem is there. The learning material and the sequencing of it *has* to be programmed, even if the student is involved in this process.

In the early 1960s educational technology was envisaged to 'revolutionize' teaching and to make schools, as they traditionally operated with graded classrooms and teachers in these classrooms giving 'frontal instruction,' obsolete institutions. In 1961, the International Congress of Applied Psychology in Copenhagen was held at the beginning of the heyday of the new pedagogical panaceas. In one of the sessions during the Copenhagen congress a series of papers were given on programmed instruction and the machines by means of which it could be given. In the discussion after the paper presentations one of the participants, apparently a teacher, anxiously asked whether the outstanding psychologists, who had spelled out the advantages of the new methods, had intended to replace teachers with machines. Robert Glaser, one of the pioneers in instructional psychology, succinctly replied: 'A teacher who can be replaced by a machine ought to'—an answer that hardly could have been more to the point.

To what extent, then, is the teacher finally going to be replaced? Before trying to answer this question about what may happen, it ought to be pointed out that formal education conducted in schools is a highly labor-intensive industry. About 80 per cent of the total recurrent expenditures are going to staff salaries. Furthermore, the costs have in all industrialized countries since the 1950s tended to go up more rapidly than the general cost of living index. The unit cost, that is to say the cost per student per year, has in some countries been almost doubled in constant prices from the late 1950s to the late 1970s. Thus, the only way of saving substantially is to reduce staff, not necessarily the teaching staff only, since the non-teaching staff in most of our countries has over the last few decades tended to grow more rapidly than the teaching force.

Before looking at the possibilities to save teaching staff one has to consider what the proper role of the school teacher really is. We tend to think that the role is fully defined as somebody in charge of planning, implementing and checking student learning. But the teacher has a central *educative* function over and above this, namely to interact, often on an individual basis, with young people in such a way so as to motivate them, help them with their individual problems and—not least—to serve as a role model. The teacher represents adult society, its values and mores, a society for which the school is supported to prepare the young. Even those students who revolt cannot do that unless they have an opportunity to revolt against people of flesh and blood. One cannot stage a revolution against a teaching machine or a computer.

In late 1967 some 150 leading educators from all over the world met in Williamsburg, Virginia to discuss the 'World Crisis in Education.' Attempts were made in the main background paper, authored by Philip Coombs (1968), and during the discussions at Williamsburg to identify the crisis symptoms and to arrive at diagnosis and cure. The imbalance between demand and supply in formal education was seen as the major problem. Various remedies were proposed, among them extensive use of educational technology, particularly in the poor developing countries. Great hopes were attached to a 'technological fix,' such as educational television which had been launched on a broad scale in, for instance, Ivory Coast in Africa. But technological innovations that even in wealthy countries had made a modest impact or no impact at all cannot be expected to work wonders in developing countries. In a paper prepared for the World Bank J. C. Eicher (1984) points out: 'New educational media (radio, television, computers and the like) are sometimes very effective but never cost effective in the context of the traditional school. Their extensive use can therefore be envisaged only as part of a sweeping educational reform or in out-of-school education programs.'

Conclusion

Given the development and complexities of modern technology and its role both in providing a desirable infrastructure and a high standard of living in modern society and in maintaining its products on the competitive international market, science is playing a key role in school education along with mathematics and communication skills. But in order to understand and assess properly the role of technology in school instruction we need to consider two basic problems which are often overlooked in conceiving what educational technology can achieve.

(1) Typically, in considering the place of educational technology, particularly the place of programmed learning, the *contextual factors* are left out, as if classroom learning takes place in a social vacuum. But what goes on in the classroom is closely dependent on the home and on society at large with its institutions. The neglect to realize this I have referred to as a 'professional disease' among teachers. In the early 1960s people involved in planning formal education in Third World countries for aid agencies, such as UNESCO, thought that educational television would be the solution to the problem of providing universal school education in Third World countries, such as Ivory Coast or Samoa. C. E. Beeby (1966) has developed a sequence of stages of teaching models which correspond to a compatible sequence of development stages in society at large.

(2) The *nature of the educative process in the school setting* has to be considered. The hopes which have been held for educational technology have often been based on the tacit assumption that school education is essentially a transmission of knowledge or a 'processing' of student 'raw material' into knowledgeable adult human beings. With another metaphor: the student is an empty glass that has to be filled up with useful knowledge. Models of industrial production have been close at hand for those who have set out to introduce innovative strategies of school teaching and to improve instruction.

But there are two features which are basic in the educative process. Its aims are by no means limited to the inculcation of certain cognitive competencies. The teaching-learning process is, as has already been pointed out, interactive, not a passive filling up with knowledge.

Education takes place in a complicated context of human relationships with parents, teachers, and other adults as well as peers. A student needs somebody to identify him or herself with. Behind this is the simple fact that cognitive competences, even though they are an important goal, are embedded in a wide range of affective goals which together constitute what we mean by character formation and personality development. In that process young people need adults to identify themselves with. They also need to become motivated by adults. Motivation cannot, in the last analysis, be created by a computer.

Thus, educational technology cannot replace the adult human beings which surround the child when he grows up and goes to school. Certain activities, like practicing reading and arithmetic, can be facilitated by technical devices but at the root of the motivation to use these teaching aids there must be an adult, in the school a teacher. We should be rather modest about what can be done by technology in a process where human contacts and motivation initiated by human beings is essential. Competencies can be inculcated only if they are carried by humanly initiated motivation.

References

Beeby, C. E. (1966) *The Quality of Education in Developing Countries.* Cambridge, Mass.: Harvard University Press.

Bell, D. (1973) *The Coming of Post-Industrial Society.* New York: Basic Books.

Comber, L. C. and J. P. Keeves (1973) *Science Education in Nineteen Countries.* Stockholm: Almqvist and Wiksell International.

Conant, J. B. (1947) *On Understanding Science.* New Haven: Yale University Press.

Cooley, W. W. and L. E. Klopfer (1961) *Test on Understanding Science (TOUS).* Princeton, NJ: Educational Testing Service.

Coombs, Ph. H. (1968) *The World Crisis in Education: A Systems Analysis.* London: Oxford University Press.

Council of Europe (1987). New Technologies and the Training of Teachers. *Western European Education.* Summer 1987. pp. 62–80.

Eicher, J. C. (1984) *Educational Costing and Financing.* World Bank Staff Working Papers, No. 550. Washington, DC: The World Bank.

Husén, T. (1974) *Talent, Equality and Meritocracy.* The Hague: Martinus Nijhoff.

Kelly, A. (1978) *Girls and Science.* Stockholm: Almqvist and Wiksell International.

Pearson, K. (1892) *The Grammar of Science.* London: Adam and Charles Black.

Rosier, M. (1987) The Second International Science Study. *Comparative Education Review*, Vol. 31:1, pp. 106–128.

Skinner, B. F. (1954) The Science of Learning and the Art of Teaching. *Harvard Educational Review.* Vol. 24, pp. 86–97.

10

Strategy Rules for Educational Reform: An International Perspective on the Spanish Situation

An Introductory Caveat

THIS CHAPTER is about my impressions of the situation in Spanish education in 1988, a situation which is still in the process of change at all levels.[1] I write this with some hesitation because most of these impressions were gathered during a visit over a couple of weeks early in 1987. Although I visited many places in the country, particularly universities, and talked to people at various levels of the educational system, from cabinet members to teachers in the classrooms, my knowledge is far too limited to permit specific observations. It would indeed be inappropriate to pass any judgment on particular institutions or specific policies in Spanish education. The chapter therefore deals entirely with generalities.

However, I am struck by the impression that many of the problems that are now besetting Spanish education are pervasive in countries in the process of reforming their educational systems. This is particularly the case if such reforms are guided by ambitions of bringing about rapid and drastic changes over a short time. In other words, when I talked to friends and colleagues in Spain about the present situation, I had a kind of *déjà-vu* feeling. What I observed in the Spanish scene fits rather well with a set of universal rules or principles that apply to educational reform, rules which I have derived from studies of school reforms over a period of forty years, in my home country of Sweden, in countries of Western Europe, and in developing countries.

No Universal Paradigms but Universal Rules

Let me emphasize right from the beginning that there are no universal

112

paradigms for conducting educational reform. Historical, cultural, and economic conditions vary so much both between and within countries that specific policies and tactics employed in planning and implementing reforms have to be considered anew for each national school system. Thus, there are no elaborate models which can be borrowed or transferred from one country to another without considerable modification. But I submit that there is a set of *general* rules that have to be followed and that these rules constitute a strategy which can succeed if taken into consideration in planning, implementing, and evaluating educational reforms. I am even inclined to go as far as to say that these rules apply to all endeavors to bring about important changes in an educational system. I have studied cases of how these rules apply when reforms are initiated by central governments. They apply in particular when radical changes affect the structure of the system and the enrollment pattern. Regulations about access to higher education, as one instance, easily stir up controversy, as has recently been the case in Spain.

I have implied above that failure to realize the importance of these principles or rules can wreck havoc with the implementation of ambitious reforms. Spain, it seems to me, has run up against so many difficulties in bringing about reforms which *per se* are highly desirable and worthwhile because, due to particular circumstances, these rules have not always been operable. This does not imply criticism of the present political leadership in any other respect than that it has perhaps been too ambitious in setting goals for sweeping reforms that are badly needed and long overdue.

Educational Reform Is Part and Parcel of Social Reform

Educational reforms have to be viewed within the context of socio-economic reforms. A corollary to this is that educational reforms cannot serve as substitutes for social and economic changes. Education, for instance, does not bring about greater social justice or changes in the quality of life. It is the other way around. The statue of Danton on Boulevard St. Germain in Paris carries the inscription: *Après le pain l'éducation est le premier besoin du peuple.* Reforms that affect the structure and content of educational provisions grow out of a need for educational opportunity that is related to improvement in the standard of living. There seems to be an inherent lawful sequence in educational reform. It is striking to note how an improved standard of living boosts aspirations for more formal education.

There is a tendency among professional educators to conceive of educational institutions as if they operated in a social vacuum. Closely related to this tendency is the idea that improved education by itself can work wonders. But education must be planned and implemented within the larger framework of socio-economic change. Conservatively inclined policymakers sometimes prefer educational reforms because they are seen as less 'dangerous' than major social and economic reforms and may even prevent the latter from occurring.

Since the 1960s, Spain has been in a period of rapid socio-economic change, with a rising standard of living for the majority of the population. Sooner or later such a society experiences rising educational demands. The process of rapid industrialization, and particularly rapid urbanization, makes inevitable, with a certain time lag, an increase in the demand for formal education with an overload in post-compulsory parts of the system. More young people stay longer in school. An 'enrollment explosion' occurs. Rural depopulation and urban growth interact to produce rising enrollments in the school system.

This is what has happened in Spain. The enormous flow of people from poor agricultural areas into metropolitan centres has resulted not only in an increase in primary school enrollment but, again with a certain time lag, an increase in secondary and higher education as well. In an agricultural society, children are contributors to the family economy. But in an industrial society with high youth unemployment, as is the case presently in Spain, the best thing is to keep the children in school as long as possible.

Reforms Cannot Be Implemented Overnight

The second universal rule or principle I would like to advance has to do with the *pace* with which a reform is carried through. Educational institutions, including schools and universities, are beset by strong institutional rigidities and inertia. Educational structures and practices are shaped by long traditions and in that process of being shaped become extremely time-honored. The fact that a new education act has been passed by a parliament and that new regulations have been issued by a government does not mean the automatic appearance of a new system of education. It takes a long time to accomplish reform. Sweden can offer one illustration.

Two government commissions into school reform were launched in Sweden in the 1940s—one expert-oriented inquiry during the first part of the decade, and one politically appointed commission during the latter part. These two commissions worked for about ten years. Then came another ten years of pilot programs which experimented with a new type of comprehensive school in a growing number of local school systems. Finally, when the Education Act of 1962 introduced the new school to the entire country, another ten years were allowed for implementation. Thus, the change took place over a thirty-year period. Fortunately, we had the same government during that period, even the same Prime Minister, which provided a background of political stability that is, needless to say, beneficial for educational reform. I shall not elaborate on this further here.

But Sweden also offers an example of a badly implemented reform in the area of higher education. The Commission on Higher Education appointed in 1968 submitted its report to the government in 1973. After the recommendations had been reviewed by various interested parties, the government passed legislation in 1975 which supposedly went into effect in 1977. I shall not deal here with the adverse consequences of this 'instant' reform. Deeply ingrained institutional patterns, like those of the universities, cannot be changed overnight.

Such experiences have taught us at least two lessons. In the first place, it is useful to launch pilot programs with sufficient time to try out new structures and curricula. Such programs can test the feasibility and soundness of the reform blueprint. Second, one should try to involve teachers, not the least by in-service training, and stimulate public debate. There is always a lot of resistance on the part of those who have an interest in the *status quo*. Their tendency is flatly to reject the reform and they are hard to involve in a dialogue.

What I have said about the need to introduce change at a slow and gradual pace applies to Spain. In recent years, it has been suffering from 'growing pains' due to the rapid changes in its social and economic fabric. No upheavals of a revolutionary nature have occurred in the society at large. When gradual changes occur in the socio-economic system, one notices that changes, with some time lag, are called for in the educational system, not the least because of the increased social demand for education in a society in the process of modernization. My point here is that educational reforms have to occur gradually if they are not going to fail completely or fade away even though they are still 'on paper.'

Resources Are Needed

A third rule has to do with *resources*, both financial and human ones. Educational reforms are very often associated with a rapid increase in enrollment at the stage subject to reform. Spain is no exception here. When more young peole stay longer in school, which occurs when education at the lower secondary level is no longer a privilege for a social and intellectual elite and becomes almost universal, the entire institution must be changed with regard to both structure and curricula. This is what has happened in most Western European countries which have changed from a socially divisive system of parallel schools to a comprehensive one that takes care of children from all social strata.

A reform by itself requires greatly increased financial resources. When reform is associated with rising enrollment, which occurs when the school-leaving age is raised, substantial increases in public resources have to be made available to cover vastly growing expenditures. In some of the highly industrialized countries studied by the Organisation for Economic and Community Development (OECD), expenditures in education grew twice as rapidly as the GNP during the 1960s and early 1980s, a period often referred to as the 'golden age' of spectacular economic growth. Under such conditions, major reforms could be financed.

However, if I have interpreted the situation in Spain correctly, the financial resources are simply not there to provide what is needed not only for current but also for capital expenditures (schools, buildings, etc.). But even if the financial resources are there, little can be achieved without sufficient numbers of qualified teachers and school administrators.

It has been said that investment in education is an enterprise with a remote time horizon. This applies, of course, in the first place to students. What the school achieves for them can be evaluated only decades later when they have reached their most 'productive' age. But in order to be able to implement a reform of the 'infrastructure' of an educational system (curriculum, methods of teaching, etc.), qualified teachers and a competent leadership have to be available. This is also a problem in Spain. It takes time to recruit and train a new generation of committed teachers who will be able to follow the reform through in the classrooms. It takes a couple of decades to assess the effects of a reform of teacher education. Changes associated with a reform require management competencies that are hard to attain even in business and industry.

This brings me to the curricular changes expected to affect classroom practices. In the late 1950s our institute in Stockholm was involved in a study of how mathematics, reading, and writing were taught in the lower secondary school. When we looked at the results, we said to ourselves that the 1919 curriculum guidelines issued by the central school authority had finally been implemented! It takes a long time to change classroom practices and it simply does not suffice to change curricular guidelines and prescriptions.

Central Government and Grassroots Participation Are Key Factors

In some countries, France and Spain for instance, the central government has traditionally had a strong hand in education. The government or the central school authority has issued regulations which have had to be rather uniformly followed all over the country. Irrespective of the degree of centralization, the experience gained in many countries is that reforms have to be initiated by a central government which also has the power to administer incentives, financial and otherwise. With few exceptions, sweeping reforms have been planned within governmental agencies and then initiated at the national level by legislation. Such legislation, however, usually affects only the general framework of an educational system, for instance, by bringing about structural changes and by putting financial resources at the disposal of local schools. Central government thereby sets the scene for changes of a more pedagogical nature (i.e., classroom teaching). In some countries, Great Britain for example, governmental commissions are set up with representatives of the various interest groups. In these commissions, blueprints for recommended changes can be worked out in a spirit of compromise. Such commissions usually try to achieve consensus with regard to major issues. Thus, a substantial amount of the preparatory reform work is conducted before people in the ministry sit down to prepare concrete legislation.

Sometimes ministries of education prepare policy documents without setting up special commissions. For instance, in 1970 in the Federal Republic of Germany the Social Democrats in co-operation with the Liberals of the Brandt government prepared what they called *Bildungsbericht 70* (Education Report 1970). This was intended as a blueprint for educational change in the Federal Republic from 1970 on. Thorough changes were envisaged through the mid-1980s, beginning with the financial resources to be made available to schools and universities. Furthermore, structural changes were to be implemented which would do away with the parallel school system after the fourth school year and make compulsory schooling comprehensive and unified. Things did not entirely work out this way, but that is another story.

The move away from planning and political decision making, including legislation, usually means a move away from the centre to the periphery, from the 'top' to the 'grassroots.' A prerequisite for a successful implementation is, as pointed out above, motivation and commitment at the local level, a motivation that can be stimulated by central incentives in the form of financial support. Participation at the grassroots level can become a problem when, as in Spain, young, energetic, and progressive 'technocrats' take over after an administration of conservative traditionalists.

Experience in many different national systems tells us that much is to be gained from achieving maximum participation on the part of those in the field who are involved in the reform. Such participation should, of course, be responsible and not merely nominal. Written submissions from interested parties and individuals can be invited. Hearings can be held with representatives of various interest groups.

It is of particular importance to open dialogue with those whose 'empires' are affected by the envisaged changes. A problem that typically occurs is that those whose roles and working conditions are strongly affected by the reform feel that things have been decided above their heads and that they do not have a fair say. At several Spanish universities, professors complained that they were not properly consulted by the

Ministry when it came to appointing committees in charge of revising the university curricula. Since they feel that their respective academic territories are strongly affected by the changes, such feelings, right or wrong, affect their motivation. Informal and motivated participation is of crucial importance both when a reform is being planned and when it is at the stage of implementation.

Educational Research and Development Is Called For

Educational reforms can gain quite a lot from being accompanied by research at the various stages, from planning through implementation to evaluation of the outcomes (Husén and Boalt, 1968). It is not possible to discuss here even in broad terms what research could do in the Spanish context. Some general observations have to suffice. I am aware of the fact that research focussed on educational problems is very limited at universities and at teacher training institutions. I am also aware of the establishment of the Center for Educational Research and Documentation (CIDE) and of what it is doing for the framing and assessment of educational policy in Spain. However, the resources for policy-oriented research have to be strengthened both at the central and regional levels, and particularly at the universities. There are two reasons for this.

First, an improved knowledge base for the framing of educational policy and the evaluation of its outcomes at the national level is called for. Longitudinal information about the social composition of enrollment in upper secondary and university education is needed in order to find out to what extent the egalitarian goals set by the government have been achieved. Continuous information about costs development is necessary for budgetary planning. Intermittent surveys of student attitudes and aspirations have to be made as inputs for realistic planning.

Second, an information system should be established both at the regional and local levels. Social councils and other bodies with governing tasks need to have access to information if they are to make rational decisions.

Some Conclusions

When the International Council for Educational Development (ICED) group of invited experts met with the Minister of Education, Dr. José Mario Maravall, in 1987, they were given a succinct definition of the problem of the educational reformer. As Dr. Maravall put it, it is one of 'bridging the gap between what *is* and what *ought* to be done.' He himself spelled out what made the gap so big in Spain, namely the void of capacity due to the restricted financial and human resources that could be allocated to education. The system, particularly at the university level, has grown so rapidly that it has left the financial capacity behind. In a period of economic crisis and austerity, envisaged reforms easily get in trouble. Institutions suffer from an overload of enrollment. Staff and buildings are lacking. On top of this, the employment prospects of those who come out of the educational system, particularly at the university level, where enrollment has increased by leaps and bounds, are rather bleak. This factor looms behind the student unrest that has occurred at secondary schools and universities in Spain. Uncertainties both among students and staff about how changes may affect their career prospects have been further exacerbated by the present austerity.

It is quite natural and understandable that an administration associated with the breakthrough of democratization in Spanish politics has been eager to change institutions that badly need to be reformed. But, as I have spelled out in this article, there are certain rules that govern change and these cannot be neglected, particularly when governments set out to change practically everything 'overnight.'

Spain now suffers from 'growing pains' related to ambitions that outpace resources and to hopes of achieving change rapidly that are being frustrated. It is to be hoped that after some years of restraint the gap between what is and what ought to be will be narrowed down. And yet in education, as in other fields of the public sector, ambitions always have to be set higher than what is actually in reach.

Note

[1]The present chapter draws heavily on observations made during a review conducted in 1987 by members of the International Council for Educational Development (ICED) who were invited by the Spanish Ministry of Education to review higher education. After the visits to various universities had been made and the review was completed, some ICED members participated in a weekend seminar organized by the Ministry of Education in Segovia, where problems connected with the reform of Spanish education at large were discussed.

References

Husén, T. (1971) Puedan las máquinas de enseñar reemplazar al maestro? *Revista de Ciencias de la Educación*, 11(4), 14–20.
Husén, T. (1972) *Origin social y educación*. Paris: OECD/CERI.
Husén, T. (1978) *La sociedad educativa*. Salamanca: Ediciones Anaya, S.A.
Husén, T. (1981) *La escuela a debate: Problemas y futuro*. Madrid: Narcea S.A. de Ediciones.
Husén, T. (1986) *The Learning Society Revisited*. Oxford: Pergamon Press.
Husén, T. and Boalt, G. (1968) *Educational research and educational change: The case of Sweden*. Stockholm and New York: Almqvist and Wiksell and John Wiley.
McNair, J. M. (1984) *Education for a changing Spain*. Manchester: Manchester University Press.
OECD (1986) *Reviews of national policies for education: Spain*. Paris. (Available also in French.)

11

From Consensus to Confrontation in British Educational Policy

THE BOOKS which have inspired this chapter all deal with central issues in the ongoing debate on British education which were raised in 'consultation papers' circulated by the British Government in 1988, but take rather different approaches in trying to come to grips with these issues. Roy Lowe's book *Education in the Post-war Years* (1988) sets out to present the 'social history' of post-war education. To a foreign observer like myself his book is indispensable in arriving at a structured picture of all the impressions obtained by direct contacts over a forty-year period of educational change. Brian Simon's *Bending the Rules: the Baker reform in education* (1988) is a downright polemical document. A reader, again such as myself, who by and large shares his ideological platform as an ardent defender of the state, tuition-free and tax-supported system of a comprehensive nature, cannot avoid finding his diagnosis of the reform bill and the analysis of its background a bit simplistic. It suffers from two limitations. The author tends to conceive British education as if it operated in a social vacuum and its problems to be inherent mainly in school and not in the society at large. Secondly, and more importantly, he does not conceive of any failings or shortcomings of the pre-Baker system and tends to regard any change as dangerous to it, a strange conservatism in a person with socialist leanings.

Take Care, Mr Baker! (1988) is a select compilation from the submissions solicited by the Government consultation papers. Julian Haviland, who has done the compilation and editing, points out in his Preface that the book is 'not intended to be hostile to either Mr Baker or his bill.' He admits, however, that objectivity has not been possible in an exercise like this, or even attempted. Anyhow, the reading of this selection of submissions conveys the impression of a massive and strong resistance in the educational establishment against the Bill. The extracts from the submissions are presented around a series of issues, such as a national curriculum, national assessment, opting out and open enrollment. It is not possible to discuss any of these issues here. But an observer from a country which traditionally has had a national curriculum much more uniform than the one envisaged in the Bill finds it difficult to understand the opposition raised against the Baker proposal in this particular respect.

Mary Warnock's book *A Common Policy for Education* (1988) should be read last, because the other three give a background to her ambition to advance a comprehensive policy for the 'revitalization' of British education. She deals with the structure of secondary education, its curriculum and examinations, as well as with the proper preparation of the teaching profession. She also takes in higher education, which directly and indirectly is affected by the new legislation.

The books are symptomatic of present trends not only in Britain but in Western Europe and America as well. Even though the British have been a bit insular in the way they have dealt with their educational problems, the present debate about the so-called Baker Reform is of interest far beyond the British Isles.

All the books appear in a situation which is far away from the consensus of the 1960s when Ministers of Education, such as Edward Boyle and Anthony Crosland, were not very far apart in their views on how British education should be modeled. Consensus has given way to confrontation and entrenchment. On the one hand we observe hard-nosed attempts to introduce practices which in the long run could end in massive privatization. On the other hand we see rigid defence of the existing state system and stubborn unwillingness to acknowledge its weaknesses as well as dogmatic rejections of attempts to initiate reform from within the system.

The British Situation: A Reform Bill in Perspective

Secondary education in Britain has been—and to some extent still is— more class-stratified than in many other Western countries. The 1944 Education Act, which formally 'democratized' secondary schooling by extending it to all children free of charge, preserved the basic divisiveness between the private and the tax-supported, state sector. For some time two issues loomed large in the British educational policy debate, namely whether or not to 'go comprehensive' and whether or not to keep the independent sector.

As a foreign observer I happened to get some insights into these issues. For instance, in August 1965 I spent a couple of days at Curzon Street with Anthony Crosland. He felt strongly committed to a reform in the comprehensive direction and was eager to hear about the Swedish experiences where we had definitely gone comprehensive all over the country some years earlier. In his book *The Future of Socialism* (1956) he wrote: 'The school system in Britian remains the most divisive, unjust and wasteful of all aspects of social equality.' The Labour government of the 1960s at an early stage decided, however, not to legislate about secondary education, but instead to try to influence local authorities to take initiatives to change. When I met Crosland in 1965 he knew about my experiences as a researcher of the Swedish reform and was keen on hearing about these experiences. He was at that time in the process of contemplating the famous Circular 10/65 and was in a quandary whether to 'request' or to 'require' that LEAs submitted plans for comprehensivization. The system was anyhow moving in that direction and the momentum grew so strong that when Margaret Thatcher took over as Minister in 1970 she did not—or could not—stop the change. Paradoxically, comprehensivization occurred more rapidly under the Conservative than under the Labour government. A right-wing group in the Conservative Party published some Black Papers issuing warnings among other things about emulating the Swedes. I was even appointed the 'demon king' of the change that had taken place in Sweden.

But educational changes are hard and slow to come by. I remember being invited to a hearing in London in the late 1960s by the Royal Commission appointed to look into the independent sector and with the charge to integrate it into the state sector. The international exchange a quarter of a century ago was otherwise rather rare in educational circles, except for referring to other countries as warning examples!

The British school system in several important respects differs from that of continental Europe. It has traditionally been much more decentralized than, for instance, in France or Sweden. Children enter school earlier. Far-reaching subject specialization in upper secondary school (sixth form) is another, rather unique, British feature.

In my role as Chairman of the International Association for the Evaluation of Educational Achievement (IEA) over many years I have been able to gain some comparative insights into how the British system performs. The comparisons are, however, limited to cognitive competence. Three pervasive observations stand out. The first is one I have made elsewhere, that 10-year olds in Britain do not perform better in, for instance, reading than their peers in other countries, in spite of entering school at least one year earlier. Scandinavian youngsters who enter at age 7 perform strangely enough at 10 at least as well, if not better, than their British counterparts. Second, at the 14 and 18 year old level British pupils on the average perform by and large as they do in other industrialized countries. At the sixth-form level they perform better in science and mathematics, which reflects the specialization mentioned above. Third, there is in Britain a much wider variation in standards achieved between schools. In spite of an acceptable average performance there is a high percentage of schools performing badly. The bottom 25 per cent are not well taken care of.

Background to the Baker Reform

Roy Lowe of the University of Birmingham sets himself the task of relating British education after the Second World War and up to the mid-1960s to the economic and social changes which took place during this period (*Education in the Post-war Years: a social history*). Deep and, indeed, 'traumatic' changes took place. The economy shifted to the tertiary sector and profound changes in family life occurred. The corporate state entered the scene. It was an era of social reconstruction and of establishing a welfare state. Lowe's central thesis is that formal education played a subordinate role in these transformations. The educational system was 'inoculated' against any revolutionary changes. There were some 'accretions' confirming existing practices instead of 'radical departures.' The elite groups by and large retained their privileges. The grand aim of the 1944 Reform that education should be 'accessible to all' was not realized during the period under Lowe's scrutiny. The vision of an egalitarian society held by, for instance, Crosland, met with many obstacles. Comprehensivization of secondary school was therefore up for a 'faltering start.' But what else could be expected during a short period of twenty years? Studies of the anatomy of educational reforms show that it takes time—and requires quite a lot of long-range political stability—to achieve in the first place the structural goals of an educational reform. Sweden presents a case in point. It had the same Prime Minister for twenty-three years! Prior to that in his role as Minister of Education he had been instrumental in initiating the reform.

Brian Simon attacks the Baker reform head on. He sees it as a massive attempt in the long run to privatize large portions of the state system and to tighten the grips of the state by undermining the influence and power of the LEA. Furthermore, the proposed Bill will dismantle an important pillar of the Welfare State. The appeal of the present British government to 'choice' and 'variety' is done away with as a 'ploy.' Of course, he has ample reason to wonder what will happen. It would, however, have been appropriate to venture a diagnosis of the British situation, the 'crisis' that by no means is limited to Britain but is shared by educational systems in almost all highly industrialized countries. Even in the highly uniform and 'socialized' Sweden there is now a mounting quest for variety and options, and this is a country with virtually no private sector at all in education. The bureaucratic 'cement cover' is heavy and increased parental influence in terms of options is called for. This deserves soul-searching and self-criticizing scrutiny.

Changes in educational policy in England today are apparently introduced in great haste. An observer with my perspective can hardly avoid the impression that the legislation prepared by the present government has been pushed through with a kind of steamroller strategy. The consultation papers circulated in mid-1987 elicited many thousands of submissions in spite of being solicited just before the vacation period, thus giving interested parties only a short time to spell out their reactions. The enormous amount of material emanating from the 'consultation' could hardly be seriously considered in preparing the Reform Bill which was presented in the late autumn. Parliament dealt with it in the spring of 1988, which was the reason for the rapid publication of at least two of the four books dealt with in this article.

Why this haste? It is, as mentioned above, one of the golden rules of reform strategies in education to let the reform process take its time. In the Swedish school reform the process of preparation was allowed many years. Problems had to be looked into thoroughly by commissions and task forces. Interested parties need to get used to new ideas and be able to discuss them thoroughly before legislation and implementation. Reforms in the educational system have to occur gradually and slowly if they are not going to fail or simply fade away without serious implementation. Institutional rigidity resists changes over night. There are many illustrations of this.

I think the DES has done itself a disservice in allowing so little time for discussion and real, time-consuming consultation. This explains the massive opposition to the Bill. Typically, Stuart Maclure who, I think, cannot be accused of not being moderate in his opinions, in his introduction to *Take Care, Mr Baker!* regards the Bill as 'fundamentally wrong.'

Mary Warnock also challenges the Baker reform, but within a broader perspective than the one adopted by Simon. She points out that there has never before been such a fierce debate over education in Britain as now. Her book, *A Common Policy for Education*, is written with the ambition to spell out a common policy for education of all children at all stages of their career. She makes a plea for a consistent policy of comprehensive schools which is not thwarted by an almost metaphysically anchored heeding of grammar school ideals. She cites Hugh Gaitskell, once a champion of comprehensive education, who said that socialism was about equality and who deeply disliked the social divisiveness of having different schools for the middle and working classes.

She conceives the educational scene in Britain to be in a 'mess' and the teaching profession to be in 'disarray,' and points out the potential conflict between education as an economic instrument and as self-development. John Dewey thought that the two could easily be reconciled, but Mary Warnock is not convinced that it would be so easy.

A central piece in the Baker reform is the shift of control from the LEA to the central government on the one hand and to the 'parents' on the other. It is a strange dual policy of 'nationalization' of control on the one hand and privatization of provisions of schooling on the other. It is interesting to note how the Reform Bill in principle runs against traditional tenets by favoring central control of how the curriculum is executed but at the same time pays at least lip-service to parental influence.

Mary Warnock is in favor of a common national curriculum but against a national assessment of the progress made by the pupils. The idea of age-related evaluation is to her the worst of all the proposals in the Reform Bill. She is sceptical of 'letting the parents in.' They are no 'experts' and are considered conservative and therefore 'unsuited' to determine the curriculum. They can form pressure groups which can make this kind of grass-root influence a doubtful prospect. Consider this kind of authority elitism in other fields of public service!

Consensus Fading Away

Similar and parallel debates about the issues raised in Britain have been going on in recent years in several other Western countries. In the United States the common, tax-supported school, for a long time regarded as a pillar of American democracy, has been put into question, and a debate about privatization has emerged. Even in a country with a monolithic system like the one in Sweden, where the comprehensive school reform in 1967 celebrated its twenty-fifth anniversary, accusations of failure have led to a debate on parental choice of schools and programmes.

The catch-phrases in the debate in Britain and elsewhere have been 'privatization,' 'variety' and 'choice.' Proposed changes in the direction of a broader variety of choices have been seen among defenders of the existing system as threats against the Welfare State and its guarantees of a minimum of equality and social justice.

Behind the criticism and disaffection with the common, maintained school among a growing number of people are two circumstances. The social problems of modern industrialized society, not least the ones besetting the family, have increasingly moved into the school, an institution primarily designed and equipped to transmit knowledge, something it can do better than other institutions. Secondly, the economy since the oil crisis and the stagflation in the early 1970s has been in a stage of austerity. The public is beginning to pose vexing questions about what it gets for the taxes spent, particularly since school expenditure in many Western countries has tended to grow considerably in real terms even though the economy at large has not done so. The proportion of adult voters with children in school, owing to demographic changes since the early 1960s in some countries, has even been cut in half, which, of course, has not added to the willingness to spend money on education.

The present system is defended and kept together by the alliance of what the Norwegian Commission on Power refers to as 'iron triangles,' interest groups consisting of politicians, unions and bureaucracies, all groups with a common interest in the public sector.

Thus, the setting is there for a confrontation superseding the consensus that by and large was behind previous legislation making provisions for nationwide educational reforms. The 1944 Education Act in Britain was supported by an overwhelming majority in both public opinion and Parliament. The 1950 and 1962 Education Acts in Sweden were passed by acclamation even voted on, although there were misgivings expressed by a few conservatives. I listened to the debate in 1950, when Prime Minister Tage Erlander took the floor and pointed out the remarkable consensus that the post-war government had been able to enlist for crucial social reforms, such as the National Health Insurance and the Family Support Act.

Is the reform in Britain to be regarded as being 'reactionary' or 'far-sighted'? One could simply avoid answering the question by saying that an answer is a matter of perception and in the long run of ideology. But I would submit that an assessment of what is happening now on the political scene has to consider the different conditions under which the school is now operating as compared to those right after the Second World War. The family has changed. For instance, far more mothers are working outside the home. We have had a massive immigration. The system has become immensely more bureaucratized; just add up the number of pages of regulations. More children stay more years in school, etc. The reforms towards comprehensivization that occurred were basically *social* and egalitarian reforms with the goal to enhance the life chances and opportunities of children from all walks of life.

In the present climate of fierce debate and entrenched confrontation we have reason to ask ourselves: who is conservative (or even reactionary) and who is progressive (or even radical)? I would maintain that the pattern of attitudes has changed in a society where the social and economic conditions in several respects are different from those at the end of the War.

Is There Any Resolution?

Mary Warnock poses the question: 'How are we to get out of the present mess?' even though she admits that there is no consensus about what education should be and what it is for. The reforms after the War aimed at making educational opportunity all the way from pre-school to the university more equal and as independent as possible of social and economic background. Reformers were faced with the task of replacing a class-stratified, divisive system with schools for different social strata running parallel to each other with a more unified and comprehensive one. The British grammar school and the German *Gymnasium* were on the

the whole reserved for a social elite. The structural changes in society at large and—not least—the enrollment 'explosion' provide, however, a new set of conditions. In the process of change schooling has increasingly become a major instrument of enhancing the life career and social status of the individual. Chances on the labor market increasingly depend on the amount of formal schooling an individual has been able to absorb. The employment system now tends to line up the job seekers according to amount of formal education and use this as the first criterion of selection. This leads to more fierce competitions within the educational system and to the emergence of the 'new underclass' consisting of those who fail and who are taking only the compulsory minimum of schooling.

Unless the 'system,' and I mean the 'maintained' system, its teachers, administrators, bureaucrats and union leaders, is not trying seriously to reform itself, parents will begin to find solutions outside the system, i.e., demand privatization. This is a core problem of representative democracy, where institutions are permeated by politics backed up by strong interest groups. Many of them were once underdogs organizing themselves in order to achieve influence and power. Having achieved power, spokesmen and bureaucracy have tended to form a 'nomenklatura,' which resists change of any kind that would reduce its power and would increase the influence of their 'clients.' In our particular case, authority officials and unions are joining hands to resist changes that would widen the margin of parental choice. Those who resist say that they are defending the interests of the children and of the weak and poor who do not possess the economic means that would give them a margin of freedom.

I do not think that those trying to 'reform' (in Britain or in some other places) are to be perceived as merely conservative or even reactionary or that those who resist change should be seen merely as defenders of progressivism and democracy. The setting is not that simple. What is at stake is the common frame of reference that a system of common schooling can provide in a working national democracy. Again, the preservation of this central feature of the majority system would require an openness and willingness on the part of the interest groups supporting 'maintained,' i.e., state education, to reform the institution from within. It requires a willingness to meet the changing conditions of schooling in a highly socially complicated, technological and information-oriented society with adequate provisions, not least by co-operating much more closely with the families. Otherwise the latter will try to establish a growing sector outside the majority system, and begin to 'opt out'—and 'privatization' will become the central issue.

There is a clash here between two fundamental views. The Government Bill advances the principle of a 'social market' in the field of school education, whereas the opposition sees education (at least during the compulsory stages) as a social service which is regarded as a citizenship right. Professor Tomlinson in Haviland's book points out that education cannot be seen as a commodity on the market to be purchased and consumed. Can a balance be struck between these two fundamentally different views? How far within a state monopoly can we let parents have a 'choice' without bringing into jeopardy values of social justice and equality of opportunity? How far should we go without jeopardizing the principle of a common frame of reference for citizens in a democratic society?

References

Crosland, A. (1956) *The Future of Socialism* (Jonathan Cape)

Haviland, J. (Ed.) (1988) *Take Care, Mr Baker!* A selection from the advice on the Government's Reform Bill which the Secretary of State for education invited but decided not to publish (London, Fourth Estate).

Lowe, R. (1988) *Education in the Post-war Years: a social history* (London and New York, Routledge and Kegan Paul).

Simon, B. (1988) *Bending the Rules: the Baker reform in education* (London, Lawrence Wishart).

Warnock, M. (1988) *A Common Policy for Education* (Oxford and New York, Oxford University Press).

12

The Need for Intellectual Coherence: The Study of History

Introduction

PROPONENTS OF educational reforms have recently been suggesting that the main preoccupation of the school should be to achieve 'literacy,' not only the traditional one of reading and writing, but scientific literacy, computer literacy, etc., as well. The common denominator of all such competencies consists of technical and analytical skills essential for participation in vocational activities.

Literacy in itself is insufficient. It has to be acquired for something that goes beyond the skills themselves. What comes to mind in a pragmatically-oriented society is, of course, the use to which literacy of various kinds can be put in working life and its role in the career of the individual. We tend to forget that the motivation behind the quest for literacy in the nineteenth century, which led to mandatory elementary school legislation on both sides of the Atlantic, was that it was indispensable for civic participation in a democratic society with franchise and elective offices. The popular movements from the end of the nineteenth century until now have been trying to provide their membership not only with improved skills in reading and writing but with basic insights which would make it possible for them to exercise an enlightened influence on civic affairs.

It is often said that education should provide the individual with the tools and insights that give him access to the culture he is sharing with other citizens in his community, country and region of the world. A disparate set of technical competencies, irrespective of whether they can be labeled basic skills or not, will not suffice in the acquisition of culture. Culture consists of the concepts and values that make it possible for an individual to have a synoptic view of the world that surrounds him and a feeling of purpose and direction in living his own life. Formal education

129

has an important, and in most cases decisive, role to play in creating the prerequisites for the acquisition of culture and in helping the individual to arrive at the synoptic view that constitutes the essence of culture. The home and community at large are both playing their important roles in this context.

Today the formal educational system, including the knowledge-generating sub-system that we refer to as research, is doing little in providing the 'cementing principles' to help young people synthesize knowledge, to structure the pieces of information conveyed to them in a mounting flow.

Those who accuse education of being inimical to culture certainly can make a strong case given the various tendencies of intellectual 'fragmentation' in today's schools and institutions of higher learning. The curriculum has become increasingly loaded with new subjects and new courses taught by specialized teachers, each distributing one carefully separated part of the intellectual fare. There is, particularly at the post-primary level, a lack of coherence in the curriculum both cross-sectionally and longitudinally. In spite of much lip-service paid to cross-disciplinarity, the various subjects are presented with little or no relationship to each other. Subjects are split up into 'courses' or 'projects.' The knowledge-generating infrastructure, represented in the first place by the universities, is becoming increasingly specialized.

What has been referred to as the 'barbarism of specialization' has led to the disappearance of the species of scholar inside or outside Academia who could be called a generalist, an intellectual who adopts a global perspective and is able to structure information in a wide field or even a variety of fields. But the generalist who has the ability 'to put it all together' has been submerged by the information revolution. If he is a university academic what counts in considering his promotion are scholarly achievements showing him as a technically skillful and creative researcher. But such achievements have more and more tended to be executed in increasingly specialized fields.

This development has had certain negative effects on the university as an intellectual community. Cross-departmental and cross-disciplinary communication has been reduced. There is not only a division between the 'two cultures,' the humanities and the natural sciences, that C. P. Snow talked about (*The Two Cultures: A Second Look* 1963; cf. Leavis, 1979) but also divisions between fields of inquiry within a set of disciplines that formally belong to the same faculty. The intellectual discourse is becoming increasingly poor in spite of all the advances made in sophisticated methodologies and the enormous accumulation of information that scholarly efforts have brought about. This discourse has tended to become more and more 'illiterate' in terms of being conducted in technical terms under a shrinking perspective.

The Emergence of 'Historical Amnesia'

I shall not deal here with how the university could tackle the problem of coping with the fragmentation that has been created by the information revolution and the increased specialization. The main concern here is what can be done in secondary school. One particular aspect of the lack of intellectual coherence or absence of synthesizing principles is the gradual disappearance of history, perhaps not in the first place from the formal curriculum but from the actual teaching.

It would be useful to begin with reviewing briefly what has brought about the present pedagogical situation of 'historical amnesia.' History was for a long time a major field of study in the schools of the Western world. It was in a way a central field of humanities and was essential in establishing cultural and national identity. In the latter respect it often contributed to the enhancement of national chauvinism. In seventeenth through nineteenth century Europe one could sometimes observe how historians systematically fueled nationalism by emphasizing the greatness and superiority of their own nations. This was often excessively done in describing the wars that allegedly had been successfully fought with neighboring countries. There was a strong reaction against this bias that made its way into history textbooks. These reactions were particularly strong after the Second World War, when various intergovernmental bodies, such as UNESCO, the Council of Europe and the Nordic Cultural Commission systematically tried to remove traces of chauvinism and what was considered to be excessive nationalism from the textbooks used in the respective countries.

Another strong movement that deeply affected the status of history as a school subject was that of progressive education, which was usually politically radical and reacted not only against the predominance of wars in history textbooks but also against the dominant role played by kings, nobility and the 'upper class' in general. The teaching of history, if any, should concentrate on the role played by 'the people,' the unknown masses, and on the social and economic forces that in various epochs molded society.

The reaction against history that consisted of 'wars and kings' went along with the quest for 'life-adjustment education.' This went along with a change in basic value orientation. According to the pragmatic tenet it would be of greater value to the student if he or she became familiar with the present-day society and its problems than with past society, which, after all, was considered underdeveloped, uncivilized and oppressive to the 'people.' Instead the focus should be on civic or social studies, expected to be a major vehicle in improving social education and education for citizenship in a reformed school. Progressive methods of teaching, for instance group work, would contribute to further such objectives. Instead of traditional 'frontal teaching,' discussions and 'projects' conducted in groups would promote social education, co-operation and group loyalty.

The progressive movement, according to which the school should take responsibility in reforming society, was not limited to the United States but had a strong influence in Europe as well. A complete restructuring of the teaching of social studies and related subject areas was expected to contribute to the attainment of the goals of the Swedish comprehensive school reforms. 'When the 1957 Governmental School Committee had to make proposals about the curriculum of the new school, and had to determine what the nine-year school had to give their pupils, it was only natural that civics was in the focus of interest' (Bromsjö, 1965). It was also expected that civics or social studies education, made 'relevant' by drawing its syllabus and activities from the society outside the school, would attract students' interest more than a subject like history with its preoccupation with the 'past.'

Studies of civic education conducted under the auspices of the IEA clearly showed that the pedagogic reality did not live up to the expectations held by those who reformed the schools (Torney, *et al.*, 1976). In the meantime the 'historical amnesia' went on. Interestingly enough, those who first and most strongly reacted against this development were young radical intellectuals. The lack of feeling of historical continuity and the concomitant ignorance about the roots of present-day society and the determinants of individual and collective identity of the person living today has inspired a renaissance of the study of history. This has gone together with reactions against extreme pragmatism and vocationalization of secondary and higher education. The study of history has again become a legitimate field of study for its own sake, a study that can help the individual establish his bearing in both time and space. Typically, in some countries geography, which for centuries had been an established field of study and an important school subject, had begun to yield to the expanding social studies courses to the extent that, as was the case in Sweden, it disappeared as a separate school subject. Cultural geography was submerged by social studies, whereas physical geography was attached to science.

The Relationship Between History and Social Studies

The study of history has in some countries tended to become almost entirely submerged in social studies. Morris Lewenstein and Rudy Tretton reviewed the situation in the State of California. They interviewed social studies department heads in twenty schools. Apart from finding that there is no such thing as a standard social studies curriculum in California, because of the immense diversification, they found that although all the schools taught American and World History this was limited mostly to one semester or less. World history, which previously was taught for one year, is losing ground and is presented within a more narrow time-frame.

The same applies to Sweden where social studies until the 1950s was taught as part of history at the secondary level. At the primary level a course in civics was given to those who had left school with the mandatory minimum of schooling (mostly seven years). In secondary school, which at that time enrolled less than 25 per cent of the students, civics was part of the history course and was taught as part of the modern history course at the end of both lower secondary (when some left school) and at the pre-university level when students obtained the certificate for university entrance. The 1946 School Commission, in drawing up guidelines for the development of the public school system in Sweden, found the curriculum to be 'cluttered' by 'obsolete knowledge' that ought to be 'weeded out' and replaced by elements that were compatible with the level of development of modern society and which provided a 'progressive orientation' (Bromsjö, 1965). Therefore, the Commission in its main report recommended that social studies should be a separate school subject and not be accommodated within history.

It would be quite inappropriate to attempt to evaluate the developments that have taken place since, say, the early 1960s with regard to the teaching of social studies. I would like here to refer to Torney et al. (1976) who present an empirical evaluation of civic education in ten countries, among them the United States. The evaluation—which is important in a subject like social studies or civics—was not confined to the cognitive outcomes but much emphasis was put on studying the non-cognitive outcomes as assessed by student attitudes and motivation.

If I should venture any generalizations from the IEA and other attempts to evaluate the teaching of social studies, I would advance the following:

(1) Social studies as a separate subject was launched and promoted with the promise that it would provide 'relevant' knowledge that appealed to the students and was to be taught with methods that were captivating. Surveys do not seem to support the high hopes that were held for this new subject area. Social studies tend to come out rather low on the 'popularity' scale. It is perceived as boring and does not catch the students' imagination. In many cases the subject matter consists of structural information about institutions which students feel do not concern them. But if the subject matter is taught in a way that superficially seems to be 'closer' to the students, the knowledge they absorb is minimal because the teaching takes on the function of entertainment, which easily adopts the character of showbusiness.

(2) Contrary to expectations, history on the average tends to be rather popular as compared with social studies. This appears to be due to the

possibilities that the teaching of history has of capturing student imagination, for instance, by depicting interesting historical personalities and concrete historical developments and processes.

How Can the School Overcome 'Historical Amnesia'?

We cannot restore the study of history as it was conducted before the 'progressive revolution.' It often consisted too much of rote learning of chronologies, too much emphasis on 'kings and wars' and too little, at least explicit, reference to what history could teach us about our present society.

When contemplating the subject area of history as being a 'synthesizer,' a study that is designed to lend intellectual coherence to what young people learn in school, we also have to consider according to what structuring principles such a study has to be conducted. It seems to me that one should try to concretize in terms of curriculum, syllabus, and methods of instruction the following:

(1) Chronological coherence and a clear sense that history is something that evolves over time and that the world we live in today has to be understood in the light of what has evolved over a long time span. Present society tends to be taken for granted and not seen as the result of what many generations have tried to achieve and influences from cultures other than our own.

A major shortcoming is the lack of a sense of continuity. Many young people today do not possess a chronological backbone for the fragmented bits and pieces of historical information that they have absorbed in school. They often have very little understanding of the enormous strides that were made socially and economically before modern society was established. A seventh-grader, who was writing a composition about Queen Christina, who in connection with her conversion to Catholicism in 1657 abdicated the Swedish throne, wrote: 'And then she took a taxi to the Central Station in order to catch the train to Rome.'

In some countries there has been among educators holding so-called progressive views on how teaching ought to be conducted strong opposition against demanding that students should learn certain key years in the chronology. The result has been that students are ignorant of important chronological milestones and on the whole have very vague notions about time sequences. These were required knowledge during the time when teachers of history were accused of indulging in 'rote learning.'

(2) The history of a young person's own region and country has to be studied along with the history of other countries, cultures and civilizations. In most countries the study of national history precedes the study of world history, the latter mainly being what in America has traditionally been referred to as the history of Western civilization. Not least in an age

of increasing global interdependence one cannot separate the study of national and international history in the way this was done earlier. Closer integration of these studies will bring about a better understanding of both the interpenetration and interdependence of various cultures.

(3) History would have to be a subject of its own, formally separated from social studies but not necessarily therefore taught in isolation from it. The main point here is that the subject has to be taught by competent teachers who are not victims of the same 'historical amnesia' as many students.

(4) The curriculum should be properly structured so as to make the students at an early stage familiar with the major stages in the development of national and world civilization. Through their entire school career they should have the opportunity to come back to these epochs again but with a deeper, more fact-loaded and sophisticated understanding. The instruction has to be compatible with the students' level of development so that the more concrete and interest-arousing aspects can be emphasized early and attempts to convey more analytical points of view introduced at a later stage. The study of literature and art should be co-ordinated with the study of political, social and economic history when students are mature for this, which usually does not occur until they are in secondary school.

What has been said here about history in school implies that this study takes a central position in what in America is referred to as the liberal arts. Whatever areas in the curriculum the various subjects belong to, they can be taught and learned in a coherent way by emphasizing the historical dimension, how human knowledge has developed and contributed to the society we have today. Until only recently there were very few university scholars involved in the study of the history of science or the history of ideas. This has changed considerably, particularly over the last decade, and ought to be seen, together with the revived interest in history among many intellectually alert young people as typical of our time and as a reaction against the ahistorical learning that has developed in schools, colleges and universities.

No other field of intellectual endeavor in school and at university has such a great potential as history when it comes to establishing the common frame of reference one is thinking of when one talks about a common culture. A major problem in a society that is multicultural and which places a high premium on pluralism is that the common frame of reference of cognitive and affective interpretations, which constitute the minimum set of common values without which a democracy cannot operate, is that pluralism leads easily to relativism and anomie. A culture presupposes that there is a system of communication that builds upon shared cognitive and affective notions. If they do not exist communication breaks down and the common culture disintegrates. That is what tends to happen in a highly overspecialized and pragmatically-oriented society, where not even the so-called intellectuals are able to communicate meaningfully.

History as the Potential for Establishing a Common Culture

History has the potential to provide the 'cementing principles' or coherence that will counteract the fragmentation and split-ups in the cognitive field of our time. It gives young people the proper perspective of the society in which they live and shows how societies, institutions and individuals change over time and how what is available today is dependent upon what earlier generations were able to achieve. The best way of teaching ecological responsibility is to show the students how the heritage from previous generations can be destroyed by greedy over-exploitation of natural resources. History is also the best device for conveying to students what in recent years has been referred to as 'global interdependence.' We have gradually become dependent on each other due both to a common past and increasing communications. Historical figures can catch the imagination of young people in whose education role models, be they historical figures, parents and teachers, play a decisive role. It is time to let the colorful personalities come back into the history books. At the core of the educative process is, after all, the influence that a role model, physically present or not, can exercise on a young person on the way to maturity.

References

Bloom, B. S. (1981) *All Our Children Learning: A Primer for Parents, Teachers, and Other Educators*. New York: McGraw-Hill.

Bromsjö, B. (1965) *Samhällskunskap som skolämne*. (Social Studies as a School Subject). Stockholm: Scandinavian University Books.

Coleman, J. S. (1982) *The Asymmetric Society*. Syracuse: Syracuse University Press.

Coleman, J. S. and Husen, T. (1984) *Becoming Adult in a Changing Society*. Paris: Organisation for Economic Co-operation and Development.

Husén, T. (1974) *Talent, Equality and Meritocracy*. The Hague: Martinus Nijhoff.

Husén, T. (1979) *The School in Question: A Comparative Study of the School and Its Future in Western Societies*. London and New York: Oxford University Press.

Husén, T. and Bromsjö, B. (1965) 'Curriculum Research in Sweden: Social Studies in Secondary Schools.' In: *Educational Research*, Vol. 7:3. pp. 165–185. London: National Foundation for Educational Research.

Leavis, F. A. (1979) *Education and the University*. London: Cambridge University Press.

OECD (1983) *Education and Work: The Views of the Young*. Paris: Organisation for Economic Co-operation and Development.

Sizer, T. (1984) *Horace's Compromise*. Boston: Houghton-Mifflin.

Snow, C. P. (1963) *The Two Cultures: A Second Look*. London: Cambridge University Press.

Teichler, U. *et al*. *Hochschulexpansion und Bedarf Der Gesellschaft*. Stuttgart: Klett.

Torney, J. V. *et al*. (1976) *Civic Education in Ten Countries: An Empirical Study*. Stockholm and New York: Almqvist and Wiksell and John Wiley (Halsted Press).

Trow, M. (1979) 'Elite and Mass Higher Education: American Models and European Realities.' In: *Research into Higher Education: Processes and Structures*. Stockholm: National Board of Universities and Colleges.

Walker, D. (1976) *The IEA Six-Subject Survey: An Empirical Study of Education in Twenty-One Countries*. Stockholm and New York: Almqvist and Wiksell and John Wiley (Halsted Press).

13

Global Learning in an
Interdependent World

A Prefatory Note

THE MAIN purpose of this chapter is to provide a background for subsequent attempts to identify and describe more concretely curricula and
programs at the undergraduate level which aim to achieve global learning.
I have tried to establish this background by reviewing (selectively) the
relevant literature and by drawing upon my experiences from the international scene as a researcher in comparative education. The focus has
mainly been on the debate about the objectives of university education in
a changing world beset by global problems, such as a new economic
order, a reappraisal of the development concept, and the danger of a
nuclear war. The ultimate aim in preparing this document has been to
bring out *central issues in university education relevant to the United Nations
University global learning concept.*

Without anticipating the discussion later in this chapter it would suffice to say here that I have quite simply conceived global learning as a
teaching-learning strategy with two main characteristics: (1) it has to do
with global problems; and (2) it takes a multidisciplinary teaching-learning approach. The modern university with its integration of the teaching
and research functions is particularly fit for a strategy of global learning
where vital problems in humankind can be tackled by a concerted inquiry
involving the whole range of disciplines.

The overriding objective of the global learning mode is to investigate in
the long run to what extent *entire nations* can learn about issues of both
national and global concern. The development of a global learning
strategy is faced with a double challenge: to take both a horizontal
approach, which means integrating knowledge across disciplines and
uniting scientific and popular experience, and a vertical approach, which
means cutting through situations at various levels: local, regional,
national and international. How, for instance, should we make local,
indigenous values and views compatible with global views and universal

values? Given the central role that universities play in the cultural life of the countries, the way undergraduate students are taught and the design of their program of learning occupy a key position in preparing the leaders of a nation.

There are dilemmas which should be kept in mind. In the first place we have the rapidly increasing specialization and fragmentation which, coupled with academic individualism, works against a cross-disciplinarity. In order to promote a cross-disciplinary approach the setting up of separate centers outside the traditional university departments has been a much practiced solution. Second, the quest for regionalization of research and teaching in higher education and the demand that priority be given to endogenous problems of Third World countries can easily come into conflict with attempts to put global problems at the top of the priority list. This means that a delicate balance would have to be struck in trying to achieve both an orientation towards global problems and proper attention to national or regional problems which badly need university assistance in order to be properly tackled.

Introductory Observations

Issues pertinent to 'global learning' were dealt with in the address given by the United Nations University Rector Soedjatmoko to the Eighth General Conference of the International Association of Universities in 1985. He pointed out the necessity for university teaching throughout the world to find a common ground in an era of increasing global interdependence. Furthermore he referred to a 'new level of complexity' of the problems shared by people all over the world. Due to the extreme specialization and bureaucratization there is a tendency in our societies to tackle each problem we encounter in isolation. Analyses of our problems tend to be unidimensional and to be conducted by specialists, in spite of the fact that these problems by their very nature are multidimensional. Those in positions of responsibility need to be able to look at problems at a higher level of conceptualization and apply integrative thinking in tackling them. The complexity and the 'avalanche of information' call for an ability to see the forest and not only the trees. What we are groping for is a new way of synthesis that professionals and those in leadership in our society should be trained to employ.

Curricula at universities in the Third World countries have usually been patterned according to European models. The 'eurocentric' system of university education has been hampering universities in these countries in their efforts to release endogenous creativity and seek their own cultural roots. There is, however, a tension between the orientation toward indigenous values and problems on the one hand and the need to address global problems on the other, a tension that can be alleviated or even resolved by communication across cultural boundaries.

Thus, university education would have to address itself to the dual task of tackling problems of global interdependence and integrative teaching and learning.

This chapter is an attempt on the basis of available material to synthesize the previous debate on how at the undergraduate level one would bring about a well-rounded general education and instill in students the ability to take an independent and integrative look at problems common to humankind. There has been an intensive policy debate, for at least a quarter-century on how to design undergraduate curricula so as to achieve such objectives.

Before the 1950s higher education was hardly a field of scholarly studies at all, which apears to be paradoxical given the fact that institutions of higher learning were the places where most of the research activities were going on. There was 'institutional research' at some American universities, in most cases studies focussed on pedagogical problems but not on universities as institutions and on the social setting within which they were operating. What has happened since the late 1960s is that higher education has become a rapidly growing field of scholarly studies. These have to a large extent been comparative in orientation. Altbach and Kelly (1985) recently published a survey and bibliography under the title *Higher Education in International Perspective* with 6,901 items, most of them from the 1970 and early 1980s. Several research centers have specialized in comparative studies in higher education. A communication network for exchange of experiences and research has been established by organizations such as International Council for Educational Development (ICED).

The Carnegie Commission on Higher Education, followed by the Carnegie Council on Policy Studies in Higher Education, dealt primarily with problems of higher education in the United States but commissioned several comparative studies. In a long series of reports it dealt at some length with problems of undergraduate education.

Given this proliferation it would be utterly presumptuous even for a relatively well-read and experienced person to present within a chapter a more detailed picture of the 'state-of-the-art' with regard to attempts in undergraduate curricula to cope with problems we here refer to as global learning. The aim is to synthesize some of the major trends in terms of policies set for universities and curricular revisions. In order to put the present situation in perspective I have provided a historical background.

It has not been my ambition to try to analyze in depth the concept of global learning. I have taken as the point of departure here the address by Rector Soedjatmoko at the IUA Meeting in August 1985. However, I have found it necessary to deal, at least cursorily, with problems of knowledge and science and different 'paradigms' used in acquiring knowledge. Michel Foucault in his book, *Les mots et les choses* (1966), points out that the way individuals organize and systematize their knowledge is determined by their culture. Each culture possesses basic codes which determine its modes of expression, perceptual schemes and patterns of actions. This has to be taken into account in dealing with the dilemma of local culture values versus attempts to arrive at a common core of global notions. A 'core curriculum' which tries to implement global learning objectives would have to be designed so as to strike a balance between localism and realization of global interdependence.

Conceptual Problems and Distinctions

Foucault's notion that knowledge is organized according to basic codes germane to the respective cultures is relevant to a discussion of the role of global learning in university education. If global learning is defined as a strategy according to which students learn about overriding global problems and acquire their knowledge in an integrative way, then one has to realize the inherent tension between the international scientific code on the one hand and the way cognizance is taken of global problems on the other. It is easy to say that university education in our time by necessity should be internationally-oriented and that students have to be made aware of pressing global problems. But the actual learning experiences can be troubled by different codes and different ideologies associated with these codes.

Traditionally universities are expected to fulfill the dual task of imparting scientific knowledge to their students and contributing to the extension of the body of scientifically valid knowledge. As shall be pointed out later the first task historically preceded the latter. Western universities were from the beginning professional schools. Research began in the seventeenth and eighteenth centuries under the aegis of the various academies, such as the Royal Society in Britain or the Academie des Sciences in France. The research university conceived by Wilhelm von Humboldt and founded in Berlin 1809 began to materialize by the mid-eighteenth century in Germany and was by the end of the century emulated in other countries, notably in Japan and the United States. The idea of the university providing service to the surrounding society was born in the United States with the Morrill Act (1862) and the ensuing establishment of the land grant colleges which contributed to the spectacular improvement of American agriculture. But it was not until recently that idea of the university accomplishing service took roots in Europe.

We shall not here try to define more precisely what should be meant by 'science' or 'knowledge.' This would lead us into a complicated (and endless) epistemological discussion. But for all practical purposes we would like to make the following distinctions. Science is constituted by the body of knowledge which according to prevailing paradigms and methodologies of 'normal science' (Kuhn) is deemed valid. Scientific knowledge is in other words the knowledge legitimized by the scientific community, as a rule by the scientific community in countries of the 'center,' a legitimacy that is meant to be accepted by those at the 'periphery.' The criteria of this community determine what should be regarded as valid and 'true' scientific knowledge. The validity is by definition universal and not confined by any cultural and national borders.

Having tried to define the body of scientific knowledge operationally by the products of the scientific community, it is evident that general knowledge goes far beyond this body. Knowledge as it pertains to everyday human affairs includes skills and conceptually organized perceptions which are closely tied to attitudes and actions. Every institution of education is involved not only in conveying verbally embedded, cognitive competencies but in changing their students' attitudes, values and beliefs as well. The trademark of university education is its emphasis on abstract, aloof and objective knowledge symbolized by the scientist at the frontier of research. But in addition to the traditional academic ethos of 'seeking the truth' university students also learn certain social roles, such as belonging to an élite or regarding politics with suspicion. Even though a separation between theory and practice, between pure and applied knowledge is emphasized and incorporated in the ethos, academics readily adopt the roles of Platonic philosopher-kings ready to provide recipes about how human and public affairs ought to be conducted. Thus even in Academia action tends to be closer to scientific knowledge than academics themselves like to think. But among the general public the two are inextricably intertwined.

Whereas academically approved, theoretical knowledge traditionally is conceived as remote from action, even to the extent of being irrelevant to practice, the *raison d'être* of practical knowledge is its applicability. Such knowledge emerges from everyday situations. It possesses a kind of *ad hoc* validity that fails to meet traditional scientific criteria. The idea that theory and practice belong to two different realms governed by two different sets of values and that they therefore should be kept separate has been a major factor in determining the predominance of theoretical competence as opposed to manual skills and competences. It explains why, not least in Third World countries, attempts to promote vocationally-oriented education relevant to the needs of these countries consistently have failed. The pressure to pursue theoretical studies as far as possible up the school ladder has been conceived as the royal road to social promotion and prestige and to powerful positions in society.

Theoretical knowledge is validated under specified restricted conditions, often under 'laboratory' constraints. The practical, 'real-life' situations are much more complicated. Many more variables are operating than in a typical experimental situation studied under strictly controlled conditions. Such a distinction between theory and practice has two important implications.

In the first place the *direct* applicability of scientifically founded, theoretical knowledge is highly limited. Such knowledge has seldom, if ever, a perfect fit with the practical circumstances where attempts are made to draw upon scientific research. In a study on the relationship between educational research and policymaking I looked at this relationship in Britain, the Federal Republic of Germany, Sweden and the United States (Husén and Kogan, eds., 1984). Policymakers who were interviewed could only point out exceptional cases where research had had a direct impact on policymaking and practice in education. The author has also collated all the information available from the some twenty countries participating in the cross-national surveys of standards achieved in a series of school subjects by students at different levels of the school system. The common denominator of the experiences of research impact was that survey findings indirectly affected policymaking either by the debate elicited by the publication of the findings or by their 'enlightenment' effect.

Second, theory and the research guided by it evolves gradually. There is ample reason to talk about 'knowledge creep.' Thus the information produced is by its very nature untimely. It is often not available when action is urgently required and therefore of limited value in coping with practical situations.

The university-trained professional is in his practical work confronted with a chaotic and dim total reality. The scientifically founded knowledge that he has absorbed at the university is not directly applicable to the problems and cases he is expected to deal with and 'solve.'

Knowledge as conceived here is not regarded in the traditional way, that is to say, as a body of verbally formulated propositions to be regarded as commodities that as other commodities can be produced, packed, and distributed. Rather, knowledge is a coping competence imbedded almost to total integration in human attitudes and human action. It is also enmeshed in history and traditions. This means that it is always beset by a tension between the local and the global. This is noticeable when so-called traditional societies are confronted with Western rationality, its science and technology and its compartmentalized and specialized competence. The most pervasive confrontation is the one between the European and North American model of formal education mediated by one of the former colonial languages. The straightforward 'linear' R&D model, developed in science and technology in the highly industrialized countries, does not apply to human and social affairs in these countries where it often has unforeseen 'side-effects.' In Third World countries the consequences can easily be disastrous. In both cases the model takes in a very limited part of the total spectrum of social and cultural reality. However, efforts have been made to avoid the side-effects, not least in United Nations University nutrition projects where the sociological aspects are taken into account.

What, then, are the implications for higher education of this sketchy analysis of the meaning of knowledge, both scientific and practical? It implies in the first place, a reappraisal of organization of undergraduate curricula in order to prepare its students to cope with 'real life' in an era of global interdependence. The reappraisal takes on an extra urgency because of the rapidly changing institutional conditions that the universities have experienced over the last few decades. Among the new auspices under which young people are educated for professional roles and eventual leadership positions are the following:

(1) Universities in the industrial countries have changed from élite to mass institutions. The same trend can be noted in some of the Third World countries. For instance, in Brazil, university enrollment increased from 80,000 to far beyond one million students in less than two decades.

(2) Increased specialization in scientific research and the ensuing compartmentalized institutionalization has led to a fragmentation of knowledge.

(3) Research has contributed to a knowledge explosion. The number of scholarly publications in certain disciplines doubles every five to six years.

(4) The division between theoretical and practical as well as between pure and applied still looms large. Those who represent 'pure' research claim that they can take no responsibility for how their research findings are used or applied. But there is growing awareness that the choice between research strategies, as well as between technologies, also is a choice between values. Attempts to develop alternative futures of energy generation, i.e., alternative energy policies, are cases in point.

(5) Specialization, and bureaucratization, of the planning and administrative functions are enhancing tendencies towards meritocracy in a society where educated ability increasingly tends to become the basis for power and influence. The gap between the ordinary citizen and the new upper class of highly educated experts tends to widen. Another consequence of particular import for the present paper is the increased need for individuals in responsible and/or leadership positions who are able 'to put it all together.'

Goals of Undergraduate Education

Against the background of cognitive competence in general and scientific competence in particular and on the changing conditions for higher education, what could be conceived as the proper goals of higher education?

The purpose of what is said here is not to espouse any particular educational philosophy but rather to try to review certain aspects of the debate that has been going on over the last century and to pinpoint programs aimed at achieving learning of a more global and integrative nature. The overview given here by no means pretends to be comprehensive but will hopefully present some of the more relevant experiences. Expressed in more conventional terms: we are here primarily interested in university programs which are internationally-oriented and at the same time try to equip students with what is referred to as liberal or general education. Some of this has been dealt with in more detail in the previous chapter.

The problems can be stated in simple terms: What traditional subjects should be included in a 'core curriculum'? Or should these traditional subjects and topical areas within them be rearranged so as to achieve the 'cross-disciplinary mix' that would prepare the students to tackle practical problems with which they will be confronted in 'real life'? Is disciplinary arranged knowledge more useful in the long run than an *ad hoc* rearrangement that helps the student to tackle actual problems but not unforeseen ones? Thus, the very exposure to problems and information relevant to their solution is a pedagogical issue of highest importance.

The pedagogical approach conducive to global learning has to be considered. Of great importance is that the 'cognitive map' in terms of specific pieces of information tends to change rapidly so as to make today's 'approved' knowledge obsolete by tomorrow. This has led to greater emphasis on cognitive skills, such as problem solving, rather than on mastery of specific facts. It has also led to emphasis on skills necessary to absorb new knowledge in an era of information explosion, and the ability to keep up with the changes taking place on the cognitive map.

A Telescoped Version of the Development of the Western University

Clark Kerr (1963) in the introductory chapter of his book *The Uses of the University* points out that the university has historically developed in 'concentric circles.' It started with philosophy in Greece and the library in Alexandria. It spread to the ancient professions and then to science. It later permeated agriculture and subsequently industry. Originally it served the élites of society, but subsequently extended its services to the middle class, and is now in the process of serving young people from all walks of life, regardless of their background.

In order to get a perspective on the Western university of today we would have to start with the Humboldtian university in Berlin, established with emphasis on research and graduate instruction which first spread to other parts of Germany and then was emulated in the United States and Japan. When Cardinal Newman in 1852 gave his famous lecture on 'The Idea of a University' making a plea for 'knowledge being its own end' and refuting the Baconian utilitarianism, the idea of research and teaching in close connection began to materialize at German universities with all the institutes and seminars which were established around university chairs.

The idea of a university where research and training of researchers was a main mission materialized at Johns Hopkins which was founded in 1876 and began as a pure graduate school with the emphasis on research. Shortly before that the Land Grant Act (The Morrill Act) had been passed in Congress, which was a breakthrough for a new utilitarian principle at the university; this was followed some decades later by the extension services which revolutionized agriculture in the United States. The young President of the University of Chicago, Robert M. Hutchins, tried to launch a 'counter-reformation' which should 'take the university back to Cardinal Newman, to Thomas Aquinas, and to Plato and Aristotle.' He succeeded, according to Kerr, in reviving the philosophical dialogue, but 'Chicago went on being a modern American university.' (Kerr, 1963, p. 17)

The undergraduate program Hutchins introduced at the University of Chicago was one designed by 'secular absolutists.' Students should be acquainted with absolute and timeless truths. Worthwhile knowledge was to a large extent embodied in a list of Great Books, which defined what every educated person should know. Thanks not least to the devoted work by the faculty and a good selection of students, the Chicago undergraduate program for quite some time was successful in training young people to become 'generalists,' by giving them a well-rounded liberal education.

Somewhat schematically we can distinguish between four models on the European North-American scenes, models that have been more or less emulated in the rest of the world:

The Humboldtian *research university* where research and teaching were expected to interact right from the beginning of university studies. Students were to gain experiences from the frontiers of knowledge, and how these frontiers were extended, in order to be prepared as pioneers in their respective professional fields.

The British *residential model*, which is the Oxbridge model built on close informal contacts between students and professors. Such contacts are considered to be every bit as important for the development of young people as is attendance of formal lectures and seminars. Such contacts have at Oxbridge been formalized by tutorials.

The French model of *les grandes écoles* epitomized a state-steered meritocratic society where professionals with a particular education are regarded as an exquisite élite. These institutions (where no research is conducted) are intellectually and socially highly selective.

The *Chicago model* was developed by Robert M. Hutchins in co-operation with Mortimer Adler. It was a program with a strong liberal-arts orientation. The ideal was to make the student familiar with the thinking of leading personalities in the humanities, sciences and the social sciences and to promote his ability to pursue further studies on his own and to train him to be independent and critical in his study and thinking.

In reviewing the development of the Western university, Kerr very succinctly sums up: 'A university anywhere can aim no higher than to be as British as possible for the sake of undergraduates, as German as possible for the sake of the graduates and the research personnel, as American as possible for the sake of the public at large—and as confused as possible for the sake of the preservation of the whole uneasy balance.' (p. 18)

Traditions of the Western University

The university as it emerged in medieval Europe over the centuries underwent few changes. It embodied the paradox of being conservative as an institution, but with regard to its intellectual orientation the hotbed of new ideas and innovations and very often of political radicalism. It was originally created to educate an élite for the church and the state. It has always at the same time tried to establish a certain amount of distance and autonomy from the power-centers. Its professors and students have tended to be a kind of guild.

Briefly the Western university has been characterized by the following:

(1) It has made distinction between theory and practice.
(2) It has put a strong premium on autonomy to the extent of complete practical irrelevance.
(3) It has, both socially and intellectually, been an élitist institution.
(4) It has been seen as an 'ivory tower,' an institution whose main purpose is to 'seek the truth.'

These four characteristics have loomed large also in universities in other regions of the world, where the European model or models have been emulated. They should therefore be spelled out a bit more in detail, not least with regard to their consequences.

On the occasion of the fiftieth anniversary of the New School for Social Research, referred to as the University-in-Exile, a special issue of the journal *Social Research* reprinted a landmark article by the outstanding political scientist Hans Morgenthau with the title 'Thought and Action.' The article is typical of how a European academic, not least a German professor, looked upon the university. Morgenthau begins his article by the following dictum: 'Theoretical thinking and action as typical modes of human behaviour are irremediably separated by way of their logical structure. Since politics is in its essence action, there exists with the same necessity an unbridgeable chasm, an eternal tension between politics and a theoretical science of politics.' (Morgenthau, 1984, p. 143). Theory tries to understand the empirical world by observing it but without changing it. Practice tries to interfere in the empirical world with the prime purpose of changing it. The *vita contemplativa*, theoretical analysis, is the very negation of the *vita activa*, political action. Morgenthau refers to the Nichomachean Ethics where Aristotle makes a distinction between *theoria* which is the highest form of human activity, not compatible with *praxis* which is part of the realm of politics.

The same views are spelled out in a more elaborate way by Professor Lobkowicz, Professor of Philosophy and Rector of the University of Munich in an anthology, *The Western University on Trial* (1983) published under the auspices of the International Council on the Future of the University (which developed as a defense against the upheaval that hit the universities on both sides of the Atlantic in the late 1960s). At the core of the 'idea of the university' Lobkowicz sees the 'pursuit of truth.' The crisis of the Western university is due to its failure to ask itself the basic question: 'What is the university good for?' The very expression 'the idea of the university' (see above) goes back to John Henry Newman in his lectures in 1852 as the founding rector of Trinity College, Dublin.

The *raison d'être* of universities is usually defended by pragmatic arguments, for instance, the competitive power of a nation on the world market. But most of the disciplines taught at the university have little, if any, direct bearing on the economic efficiency of a country and its standing in international trade and military competition. Its faculty and researchers feel an obligation to contribute to the extending of the frontiers of knowledge which they see as its fundamental and distinctive mission.

A university is a comprehensive institution with a wide range of disciplines and specialities. The very multiplicity of subjects enables the university to combine professional training with cultural enlightenment. The fact that humanities, social sciences and natural sciences are studied in the same institution enables it to educate well-rounded professionals and not just narrow technocrats. It is particularly important to bridge the gap between humanists and scientists, the 'two cultures' to which C. P. Snow referred in *The Two Cultures: A Second Look* (1963).

'The university, as originally conceived, is the only human association in which men can come together solely for the purpose of knowing ... [it] represents institutionalized theory.' (Lobkowicz, p. 34) The search for truth is what ultimately justifies the existence of a university.

According to this view the university serves society best by being itself a 'place for tranquil, disciplined and objective thinking,' which is the best way of preparing for *any* profession.

Most of those advocating what could be called the ivory tower model of a university agree that the university should serve society by pursuing things that are not necessarily relevant to that society. Such functions, they say, can also, and more effectively, be fulfilled by other institutions which are not distracted from their pragmatic tasks by studies that are justified only by their cultural nature and which require a high level of originality and detachment from practical concerns.

The traditional European philosophy about the proper role of the university has had strongholds at the great research institutions and, on the whole, at élite universities. But not even at those institutions, depending upon how they perceive their mission, has this philosophy gone unchallenged. One example is Massachusetts Institute of Technology which for a long time has contributed to policymaking in the United States in both technology and economics. The stance expressed by, for instance, Morgenthau has increasingly been repudiated by academics determined to break away from the idealistic philosophy of a demarcation line between *theoria* and *praxis*. A similar development can be seen in the Third World countries where the role of universities in promoting social and economic development has become a major task (see, for instance, Thompson *et al.*, 1977). In this study the focus was on 'promising experiments' going on in LDCs with the purpose of having higher education play a pivotal role in social change.

Upheaval and Critique

What is referred to above as the ivory tower view has been challenged during the last few decades. The 'ecology' of higher education has changed rapidly since the early 1950s. Enrollment in the industrial countries has multiplied many times. Universities thereby have changed from élite to mass institutions (Trow, 1973). Research began to be supported by governments on a massive scale to the extent that one began to talk about Big Science. The increased financial support from public sources gave rise to demands for accountability and influence on the part of public interest groups on university governance. Whether the academics wanted it or not, they became closely involved with government and industry, not least by undertaking large-scale commissioned projects. New areas of study were drawn into research. The 'scientification' (*Verwissenschaftligung*) created hopes that research would add a new dimension of rationality to decision-making in public affairs. The hopes were high for what science could achieve in improving human conditions, see, e.g., Lundberg *Can Science Save Us?* (1947). The tendency to 'vocationalize' university education, at a time when there was more demand for the existing supply of highly trained manpower, was met by opposition on the part of students who also reacted against the neglect they felt they were subjected to in an era of rapidly increasing resources for research, with professors caring more about their research projects than about their teaching.

The uproar at the University of Paris in early 1968 was illustrative of what happens when student disenchantment reaches an explosive level. The minister of Education Edgar Faure, the architect of the 'guideline legislation' (*loi d'orientation*), has spelled out his diagnosis of the French situation and the objectives of the law in his book *La philosophie d'une réforme* (1969). He has in the book collected the presentations given in the National Assembly and at the UNESCO General Conference in the fall of 1968. He regarded the 1968 student upheaval as a crisis of communication at the root of which, from a political point of view, was the double problem of autonomy and participation. He quotes a UNESCO report according to which young people through modern news media learn to know about different cultures and tend to form a separate international youth culture which opposes adult cultures locked into traditional schemes. This was a youth in revolt which was aware of Vietnam and genocide, and who violently opposed the consumer society which tended to deprive the individual of his self-control.

Faure also pointed out the lack of balance between faculties and disciplines in terms of enrollment. In France, six students out of ten were in the humanities and the social sciences and only one out of four in the natural sciences. The planning document prepared by *Commissariat du Plan* called for at least twice as many in science.

Faure also hinted at the powerful influence of the traditional idea of a 'culture générale,' a classical education provided to a limited number of students. The functioning of the modern mind depends heavily on the 'languages of our time,' science and technology, not primarily on Latin and Greek, which were center pieces in the traditional notion of 'culture générale.' The new university, guided by the principles of autonomy and participation, needed a new pedagogy based on dialogue and just transfer of knowledge, which, once it had accumulated to a certain stock, was assessed by 'punctual examinations.' Furthermore, universities should realize that team work was called for, because in the real world this was a basic mode of work not least in management. The new category of students who to a large extent came from homes without a tradition of high-level education would gain most from such changes. These would also have to be enhanced by putting emphasis on learning how to learn in university courses as well as by injections given to the teachers on how to teach.

Reappraisal of the Role of Higher Education in Development

The Western universities went through a period of soul-searching self-examination after the period of trials and tribulations which reached a peak with 'the events' (*les événements*) of 1968. Those who defended the traditional idea of the university felt that it was under fire by those who wanted to politicize, moralize and reform an institution whose 'primary allegiance is to cognitive rationality' (Chapman, 1983, p. 1).

The re-examination was also partly one of epistemology. Much of the quest for a hermeneutic approach was a revulsion against the analytic and utilitarian rationalism and a call for spiritual unity and moral significance. There was here, of course, an internal ambiguity between the two approaches which required a delicate balance to be found. It was felt that the Western universities, primarily committed to intellectual objectivity, and in their internal promotion using the criterion of competitive excellence, were not quite adequate to meet the needs of the Third World countries.

Agencies concerned with human and social development took a much more pragmatic view of the role of universities in Third World countries. UNESCO noted that science, being a product of history and society, 'owes as much to the social environment as to the work of scientists.' Science interacting with the surrounding society leads to the conclusion that the developing societies should try to work out their own scientific and technological development strategies. Although on a long-term basis the application of science calls for analyses of global problems it has to recognize the importance of local cultures and the needs of the people who share that culture. In its Medium-Term plan for 1977–82 the agency pointed out that the new concept of development puts the person at the center of development. A major objective should be 'promotion of the formulation of a global, multidisciplinary interpretation of development, having regard to the interrelations between the various factors contributing to this and which are, in return, affected by it.' In a presentation to an African audience, the Director-General pointed out that in the developing countries the university has a key role, where students and teachers from a wide variety of background can work together 'combining training and research, study and production, tradition and progress, attachment to one's identity and responsiveness to the world, in the work of pursuing the objectives of the community.' (Sanyal, 1983, p. 8) Within the UNESCO Medium-Term Plan the Division of Higher Education adopted certain principles of action, among them giving priority in higher education to endogenous national development, avoiding élitism and giving national policies precedence over individual option, and promoting institutional co-operation which could be used to bridge the gap between countries at different stages of development.

Foreign Study and the 'Globalization' of Perspectives

Worldwide, the number of students attending universities outside their home countries has increased eightfold over a period of thirty years. The motive to study in foreign countries is in the first place to get a good professional training which either cannot be obtained in the home country, or if available, is considered inferior to the one available in the host country. But beyond that, graduate study at leading institutions in other countries is a means of transferring competence and knowledge essential for the economic and social development in the home country. Study abroad has been an 'appropriate educational fix for the human capital needs of developing countries.'

Even though foreign study has gone through a period of spectacular expansion over the last few decades it has a long history. Leading universities established themselves on the European continent much earlier than in countries on the periphery where they were unable to reach the level of quality of the continental ones. Students from peripheral countries flocked to the universities in Germany and France. Latin served as the *lingua franca* and had the same instrumental value for international communication in the scholarly world as English and French have today.

In addition to the pragmatic goal of obtaining a useful professional training a period of study abroad can contribute to broadening the cross-cultural perspective. A deepened knowledge of the human conditions in other cultures contributes to the promotion of international discourse and understanding. It would run counter to all we know about the psychological origins of human conflicts if foreign study did not have such effects. The various aspects of foreign study have been dealt with in a special issue (Vol. 28:2, 1984) of the *Comparative Education Review*. In introducing the issue the editors point out that 'insufficient scholarly attention has been devoted to foreign study and its manifestations.' (*op. cit.*, p. 167) Until the early 1970s, there was the belief in the international and other agencies dealing with development education that higher education was the key to an economic 'take-off' in countries newly freed from colonial rule. A few, highly trained, individuals would have a 'multiplier effect' and would bring about a take-off in the educational system as well. Foreign study would be the fastest route to replacing highly trained expatriate manpower and making provisions for a rapid economic development.

In the 1970s there was a shift in the priorities, noticeable for instance in the World Bank's educational policy which changed from providing primarily post-secondary education to meeting in the first place the basic educational needs of the poor in Third World countries. At the same time doubts were being raised about the value of the advanced higher education provided at leading universities in the North. The categories of thinking imparted at foreign universities were those of 'normal science' in these countries. The relevance of the subject-matter presented and the frame-of-reference for it was called in question. Students from developing countries coming to 'center' countries for graduate studies were incorporated into the scientific-technological infrastructure of these countries dominated by market economies. Underlying all this were the epistemological and philosophical foundations of the Western countries with a research orientation and attitudes towards teaching and curricula reflecting a highly developed and affluent economy. The outcome of all this was emulation of the professional models of countries in the 'center.' This does not always work in the direction of liberating indigenous creativity and self-reliance.

Given the background that has just been hinted at, the very idea of foreign studies in so-called 'center countries' has been challenged (e.g., Weiler, 1984). Weiler sees the dependence on academic training provided by center countries as 'the more significant obstacle to cultural authenticity.' (*op. cit.*, p. 177). We are here faced with a serious dilemma which for quite some time will loom large. How can very bright students from developing countries be given opportunity to develop their potential without being sent to top 'center' universities?

How can cultural authenticity and the cultivation of local and/or national traditions and paradigms of inquiry be made compatible with the quest for 'globalism' in higher education which has become urgent in a world of increasing interdependence? The modes of inquiry and the entire intellectual orientation have by tradition since the seventeenth century been universal in character. Scholars have been searching for universal truths and universally valid principles. As pointed out above, Latin was, in spite of wide linguistic, cultural and other differences, the language of scholarly communication. Students from the backward and underdeveloped countries in the North went to Paris, Prague and Leyden for their studies which were mediated by Latin. One could easily find parallels in earlier centuries to countries in the 'center' and 'periphery' respectively.

The idea of the university as it still is espoused in Europe and North America has dominated Western science. In considering the predicament of Western universities by 1980, in his Introduction to *The Western University on Trial* (1983), Professor Chapman, political scientist, points out: 'No other civilization—not the Chinese, Indian, or Islamic—invented an institution specialized for intellectual education; this is unique to the West' (*op. cit.*, p. 1). But he is strongly aware of the tension between individualistic rationality and the desire for spirited unity and moral significance. This internal ambiguity calls for a delicate balance between truth seeking and relevance.

Jan Amos Comenius, leading educational reformer in seventeenth century Europe, was convinced that the main prerequisite for educational reforms of international proportion was a common language of instruction in higher education. To this effect he prepared his *Janua linguarum reserata* (The Door to the Languages Opened) which came out in 1631. It had a phenomenal success and was published in twelve European languages as well as in Arabic, Persian and Mongolian. Alfred North Whitehead once referred to the seventeenth century as the 'century of genius' with outstanding scientists, such as Bacon, Galileo, Kepler and Locke. He could just as well have referred to it as the century of genius in the realm of international relations, where scientists and philosophers were able to communicate with each other through the *bona officia* of the new academies, such as Royal Society in Britain or the Academie Royale des Sciences in France. Intellectual communications were established between scholars in Europe and the Far East. Along with internationalism went growing pluralism and religious toleration in countries like the Netherlands which was further spurred by expulsion of religious dissenters from other countries. In order to understand the preoccupation of Comenius with peace and international understanding, tolerance and education for pluralism, one has to consider a Europe plagued by lengthy and devastating wars.

Internationalism in the seventeenth century was marked by more than a dozen proposals for a universal language. There was almost the same number of cultural Utopias and schemes for educational co-operation, such as Bengt Skytte's 'Sophopolis' (Brickman, 1983–84), where, inspired by Comenius, he spelled out the idea of establishing centers or cities of learned and wise men drawn from many countries. Such centers were conceived as islands of tolerance, and bulwarks against censorship and persecution. At least two universities, the ones in Padua and Leyden, had multinational faculties and student bodies. The idea of cross-national co-operation in culture, science and, not least, in education, was indeed a hallmark of the seventeenth century. Francis Bacon in *Solomon's House* developed a plan for such co-operation.

The Undergraduate Curriculum[1]

Curriculum refers to the rationally ordered structure that guides the learning process of students. Such structures determine the priorities and the sequence of the various elements that constitute a given body of learning. Thus a curriculum can be defined as a technique whereby human thought is ordered for the purpose of transmitting knowledge. In his Foreword to Frederick Rudolph's *Curriculum: A History of the Ameri-*

can Undergraduate Course of Study since 1636 (1977) Clark Kerr offers this definition: 'In the final analysis, the curriculum is nothing less than the statement a college makes about what, out of the totality of man's constantly growing knowledge and experience, is considered useful, appropriate, or relevant to the lives of educated men and women at a certain point in time.' (*op. cit.*, p. ix)

Before the age of Enlightenment, both the school and university curriculum was based on faith, reverence for the past and firm trust in authority. Already before the impact of the century of Enlightenment a change was elicited by the Cartesian mode of thought, which proceeded with Newton and was completed with the Encyclopedists, a development leading up to nineteenth century positivism. Even though the dominance of the Scriptures subsided, for a long time the classical heritage, with Latin and Greek playing key roles, prevailed. Classical studies were considered to constitute the core of *culture génerale*.

Kerr points out that in order to get a proper perspective on today's undergraduate curriculum in the United States, one has to compare it with 'the highly prescribed curriculum of the first American colleges, to the classical curriculum defended by the Yale Report of 1828, to the elective curriculum adopted at Harvard in the 1870s and its modifications in 1909, to the comprehensive university created at Cornell in the 1860s and the research university created at Johns Hopkins in the 1870s, and to the many experiments with core courses, interdisciplinary education, and competency-based learning that have taken place in our present century.' (*op. cit.*, p. ix)

The change which took place in the undergraduate curriculum in the United States at the end of the nineteenth century, for instance with President Charles Eliot's inaugural speech at Harvard in 1869, paved the way for a liberal arts undergraduate curriculum at leading institutions. It was emphasized that young people should have 'an accurate general knowledge of all the main subjects of human interest.' Eliot's successor Lowell, who took office in 1909, defined liberal education as an attempt to give the studies both depth and breadth.

A curriculum is often perceived in terms of what subjects should be studied for how many years and periods per week, and what topics within each subject area should be in what sequence. The choice of subject areas and their relative importance reflected in how much teaching should be devoted to them is usually controversial, because it has to do with the relative importance and power of various academic organizations. Thus territorial fights easily flame up. The problem of composing a well-rounded curriculum becomes particularly difficult and vexing because the academic reward system promotes narrow specialization and therefore works against cross-disciplinary approaches necessary for a concerted effort in tackling real life problems.

But there are also difficulties in trying to achieve a consensus about what subjects should constitute the 'core curriculum' in studies organized to achieve the aims of a 'liberal' or 'general' education. Evidently, if an institution of higher learning wants to turn out graduates with a well-rounded education, which has the dual aim of preparing them both as professionals and as educated people, a tough selection among the *smorgasbord* of courses offered by perhaps some fifty or more university departments has to be made. Each of these departments are offering many courses out of which a selection has to be made. This enormous variety of courses, each with a rather diluted body of information, easily leads to a multidisciplinary illiteracy. Superficial knowledge replaces study in depth, and the great many small courses easily prevent the development of analytical skills of criticism, independent study which is a by-product of every study in depth.

Harvard University on two occasions, in 1943 and 1978, has appointed committees with the charge of inquiring into the problem of devising a curriculum of well-rounded general education for undergraduates.

The 'Red Book,' the 1946 report of the 1943 Committee on 'General Education in a Free Society,' went to some length to put the issues of undergraduate curriculum into the framework of modern, democratic society. Given its premises, democracy evidently carries the germ of 'discord and even to fundamental divergence of standards.' On the other hand democracy cannot function unless there are some 'binding ties of common standards.' This dilemma has to be resolved by the educational institutions who have to contribute to a common frame of reference of standards and beliefs without which democracy cannot survive.

The undergraduate curriculum would have to reconcile opposite objectives: heritage and change, communality and diversity in outlook. In their discussion of the principles upon which a core curriculum 'for survival' should be based, Boyer and Kaplan (1977) point out that every core curriculum in the past has been guided by a vision of communality. To be sure, all the students should be equipped with some basic, disciplinary competence. But they should also learn to be self-aware in relation to tradition. This goes beyond 'knowing,' it means knowing *how* and *why* we know. The core curriculum that Boyer and Kaplan propose is 'built on the proposition that students should be encouraged to investigate how we are one as well as many.' (*e pluribus unum*, p. 58)

What do they consider to be the communality, the 'core' of a common undergraduate 'survival' curriculum? The curriculum should embrace three domains: (1) History that makes students aware and knowledgeable about the common heritage, a history taught without bias and with a minimum of national ideology. (2) Exposure to the broad range of issues raised by our common existence. This means 'comprehensive literacy' in terms of various 'languages,' including mother tongue, computer language and mathematics. It also means studies of institutions in our present society and their impact on the individual. In addition, the roles we play as producers and consumers need to be studied. (3) Preparation for the future on the basis of knowledge about the present situation. Depletion of natural resources, proliferation of nuclear weapons, overcrowding and mass starvation, unbalanced distribution of economic resources, are some of the problems in a world of increasing interdependence. 'Global destinies, once having arrived collectively at some irretrievable, unmanageable point, cannot then be reversed to some earlier moment of sanity.' (p. 72)

The second Harvard committee was chaired by the Dean of Arts and Sciences, Henry Rosovsky. In 1978 it produced a report under the title 'Report on Core Curriculum.' Out of one hundred courses the committee proposed a selection of eight with the intent of arming the undergraduates with a common learning but *not* with a body of common teaching. The committee proposed that every undergraduate student should take at least one course in each of the following areas: (1) literature and arts, (2) history, (3) social and philosophical analysis, and (4) foreign languages and cultures. The teaching and learning in these fields should put particular emphasis on the 'mode of understanding' in the respective fields.

Those who have participated in the discussion about the core curriculum have pointed out the importance of putting emphasis on the *modes of inquiry* in the major fields of intellectual discourse instead of trying to present comprehensive courses with a big load of more or less unstructured and undiscussed information.

Dilemmas in the Preparation of Undergraduate Curricula

In preparing its curricula the university is faced with the classical duality of tasks: on the one hand it is expected to prepare for research and generation of new knowledge; on the other, it is in charge of reproducing already existing knowledge to a new generation of professionals. These two main tasks easily come in conflict with each other, since most of the young people who are not heading for research positions are not interested in research and those aiming for a research career are more interested in transforming instead of accepting existing knowledge.

Another dilemma has to do with specialization versus comprehensive overviews. Evidently a study in depth in a given field generates solid competence in that particular field but easily leads to a narrow-minded outlook and weakens the ability to learn new things when the subject matter becomes obsolete. A solution to this dilemma has been to recommend a common core curriculum or a 'liberal-arts' curriculum which provides a common background or frame of reference for all students. It gives all students an opportunity to test their interests and abilities and can thereby serve as a launching pad for subsequent specialization. The danger of too much specialization at the undergraduate level has been given quite a lot of attention. But considering the exponential growth of research coupled to an enormous specialization (reflected in the rapid growth of the number of specialized journals) there is also ample reason to be concerned about too much one-sided specialization at the graduate (doctoral) level.

A well-rounded general education is concerned not only with cognitive objectives but with emotional and moral development as well. It has to do with cultivation of values. When in 1943 President James Conant of Harvard University appointed a committee on 'General Education in a Free Society,' with the charge to look into the proper curriculum for the 'great majority' and not only the 'comparatively small minority which attends the universities or colleges,' he said in the Introduction to the Report submitted in 1945:

The heart of the problem of a general education is the continuance of the liberal and humane tradition. Neither the mere acquisition of information nor the development of special skills and talents can give the broad basis for understanding which is essential if our civilization is to be preserved. No one wishes to disparage the importance of being 'well informed.' But even a good grounding in mathematics and the physical and biological sciences, combined with an ability to read and write several foreign languages, does not provide sufficient educational background for citizens of a free nation. For such a program lacks contact with both man's emotional experience as an individual and his practical experience as a gregarious animal. It includes little of what was once known as 'the wisdom of the ages,' and might nowadays be described as 'our cultural pattern.' It includes no history, no art, no literature, no philosophy. Unless the educational process includes *at each level of maturity* some continuing contact with those fields. It must fall short of the ideal. The student in high school, in college, and in graduate school must be concerned, in part at least, with the words 'right' and 'wrong' in both the ethical and the mathematical sense. Unless he feels the import of those general ideas and aspirations which have been a deep moving force in the lives of men, he runs the risk of partial blindness (pp. viii–ix).

This was said before the post-war enrollment explosion had begun in the United States, not to mention Europe. But the massification at the undergraduate level with the wide variability among students in background, intellectual ability, interests and expectations created a situation where major changes were called for. One of the strategies developed to cope with the new situation was the establishment of the comprehensive university, the 'multiversity' in the term coined by Clark Kerr in his famous Godkin lectures in 1963, or the *Gesamthochschule* that hardly took off in Germany after the turmoils of the late 1960s and early 1970s. The establishment of the comprehensive university occurred with various motives. In the Swedish U68 reform bringing all students into big comprehensive institutions of higher learning a *högskola* was considered to possess the same virtues as comprehensive secondary schools, namely, in addition to providing a common frame of reference, one would also be able better to achieve egalitarian values. By integrating the heterogeneous student body into one institution, one would use this variety as a stimulus for learning.

Closely related to the comprehensive approach as a response to massification were the systematic attempts to vocationalize programs, particularly those in the faculties of arts and sciences. Every university program should lead to a given vocational sector, which, for instance, was the case in Sweden. Attempts were made in this context to disconnect teaching from its disciplinary orientation and to incorporate problem-solving approaches as learning styles.

It is perhaps too early to pass more definitive judgment about the policy of the comprehensive institutions introduced in Europe in the 1970s. As pointed out by Ladislav Cerych in a paper on 'Retreat from ambitious goals?,' (1980) there has been an 'appreciable loss of momentum in certain ambitious reforms' and the late 1970s have been a period of 'reform dissolution.' He makes particular reference to the French 'orientation law' of 1968. What he is referring to in essence is a time-honored experience: namely that one cannot overnight change institutions that have existed over many centuries.

Issues Confronted in Establishing a Global Learning Strategy

A balance has to be struck between, on the one hand, endogenous creativity and independence of the dominant intellectual streams from Europe and North America and, on the other, the universalistic orientation in science and technology in attempts to tackle pressing global problems.

Universities in Third World countries both in their teaching and research have to address social and human development in their own regions and countries but also have to open the perspectives of their students to problems of a universal character. This, again, requires a delicate balance between parochialism and internationalism.

A balance has also to be struck between, on the one hand, reductionistic solutions to complex problems (and the intellectual intolerance and authoritarianism that goes with it), and, on the other, pluralism in approach, criticism and openness to new ideas and perspectives which constitute a climate of flexibility in teaching and research.

Research paradigms, particularly in the social sciences, with their 'imperialistic character' demanding the submission of traditions and values rooted in the indigenous culture have to be balanced against cultural authenticity.

The academic ethos at Western universities according to which the overriding objective of the university is 'to seek the truth,' an activity seen as separate from the total responsibility for social and human affairs of the surrounding society or the world as a whole, represents an issue which has become particularly burning in modern societies, with their close relationships to research. This issue is closely related to the dichotomy between theory and practice.

Universities are institutions where the majority of future national leaders are educated. It is in the nature of the level of teaching ('higher education') and its relationships with new knowledge (which is not always easy to master) that they become élite institutions. They, therefore, to a varying degree easily become intellectually and socially selective. It is often in the interest of the élite, particularly in a meritocratic society, to guard its power by restricting access to élite institutions (see for instance *les grandes écoles* in France).

General versus specialized education is at the core of the problem of establishing favorable auspices for global learning. The solution is not to provide comprehensive survey courses in the various faculties; the core of the matter is the *style of learning* one adopts. It is a learning that goes far beyond any encyclopedic definition of relevant knowledge in a particular field. It has to do with skills, values and beliefs, etc.

Global learning means focus on global issues and the learning needs which are associated with them. The extent to which such issues are addressed is a test of the quality and adequacy of the formal education which is at the center of what is referred to as 'liberal education.'

Note

[1]It is out of question here even to try to synthesize the main studies, historical and others, of university curricula in various parts of the world. Not least thanks to the thorough work of the Carnegie Commission on Higher Education the curricular development at American colleges and universities are the best known.

References

Altbach, P. G. (Ed.) (1975) *The University's Response to Societal Demands.* New York: International Council for Educational Development.

Altbach, P. G. and David H. Kelly (1985) *Higher Education in International Perspective: A Survey and Bibliography.* London and New York: Mansell Publishing Ltd.

Beichman, A. (1983) Is Higher Education in the Dark Ages? *The New York Times Magazine,* November 6, 1983.

Ben-David, J. (1977) *Centers of Learning: Britain, France, Germany, United States.* New York: McGraw-Hill.

Bergendal, G. (1981) *Higher Education and Knowledge Policy: A Personal View.* Malmoe: School of Education.

Bergendal, G. (1983–84) Knowledge Traditions in Higher Education. *Western European Education.* Vol. XV:4, Winter 1983–84.

Blackburn, R. *et al.* (1976) *Changing Practices in Undergraduate Education.* Berkeley, Calif.: Carnegie Council for Policy Studies in Higher Education.

Botkin, J. W., M. Elmandjra and M. Malitza (1979) *No Limits to Learning: Bridging the Human Gap.* Oxford: Pergamon Press.

Boyer, E. L. and M. Kaplan (1977) *Educating for Survival.* Change Magazine Press.

Brickman, W. W. (1983–84) Swedish Supernationalist in Education, Science and Culture: Bengt Skytte (1614–1683). *Western European Education*, Vol. XV:4, Winter 1983–84.

Burn, B. B. (1980) *Expanding the International Dimension of Higher Education*. San Francisco: Jossey-Bass.

Cerych, L. (1980) Retreat from Ambitious Goals? *European Journal of Education*, Vol. 15:1, May 1980.

Chapman, J. W. (Ed.) (1983) *The Western University on Trial*. Berkeley: University of California Press.

Chait, E. F. (1975) *The Useful Arts and the Liberal Tradition*. New York: McGraw-Hill.

Comparative Education Review. Special Issue: Foreign Students in Comparative Perspective. Vol. 28:2, May 1984. University of Chicago Press.

Dirks, W. *et al.* (1983) *Existenzwissen*. Frankfurter Hefte, Extra 5. Frankfurt: Neue Verlagsgesellschaft.

European and American Universities—Their Responsibilities at the End of the 20th Century. Report from Aspen Institute Berlin 1984. Berlin: Aspen Institute for Humanistic Studies. Report No. 4, 1984.

Faure, E. (1969) *La philosophie d'une réforme*. Paris: Pont.

Faure, E. *et al.* (1972) *Learning to be*. Paris: UNESCO.

Foucalt, M. (1966) *Les mots et les choses*. Paris: Gallimard.

General Education in a Free Society. Report of the Harvard Committee. (1945) With An Introduction by James Bryant Conant. Cambridge, Mass.: Harvard University Press.

Heilbronner, R. L. (1974) *An Inquiry into the Human Prospect*. New York: Norton and Co.

Husén, T. (1979) General Theories in Education: A Twenty-Five Year Perspective. *International Review of Education*. Vol. 25.

Husén, T. (1980) A Marriage to Higher Education. *Journal of Higher Education*. Vol. 51:6.

Husén, T. (1985) International Education. *International Encyclopedia of Education: Research and Studies*. Oxford: Pergamon Press.

Husén, T. (1986) *The Learning Society Revisited*. Oxford: Pergamon Press.

Husén, T. and M. Kogan (Eds.) (1984) *Educational Research and Policy: How Do They Relate?* Oxford: Pergamon Press.

Hutchins, R. M. (1969) *The Learning Society*. New York: Praeger.

Inkeles, A. and L. Sirowy (1985) Convergent and Divergent Trends in National Educational Systems. *Social Forces: An International Journal of Social Research*. Vol. 62:2.

Jencks, C. and D. Riesman (1968) *The Academic Revolution*. New York: Doubleday.

Kaysen, C. (Ed.) (1973) *Content and Context: Essays on College Education*. New York: McGraw-Hill.

Kerr, C. (1963) *The Uses of the University*. New York: Harper and Row.

Kuhn, T. (1962) *The Structure of Scientific Revolutions*. Chicago: University of Chicago Press.

Levine, A. (1978) *Handbook on Undergraduate Curriculum*. San Francisco: Jossey-Bass.

Lobkowicz, N. (1983) Man, Pursuit of Truth and the University. In: John W. Chapman (Ed.) *The Western University on Trial*. Berkeley: University of California Press.

Lundberg, G. A. (1947) *Can Science Save Us?* New York: Longmans, Green and Co.

Morgenthau, H. (1984) Thought and Action in Politics. *Social Research 50th Anniversary*. New York: New School for Social Research.

Muller, R. (1985) A World Core Curriculum. In: Yogendra, Vijayadev (1985) *Future Education*. Warwick, Australia: Centre Publications.

Neave, G. (Ed.) (1978) *Recession and Retrenchment*. Review of New Trends in European Higher Education. Special issue of *Paedagogica Europaea*. Vol. 13:1.

Newman, J. H. (1947) *The Idea of a University*. New York: Longmans, Green and Co.

Prospects. Quarterly Review of Education. Vol. III:4, Winter 1973. Special Issue on the European University in Change.

Riesman, D. (1980) *On Higher Education*. San Francisco: Jossey-Bass.

Rosengren, F. H. *et al.* (1983) *Internationalizing Your School*. New York: National Council on Foreign Language and International Studies.

Rudolph, F. (1977) *Curriculum: A History of the American Undergraduate Course of Study Since 1636*. New York: McGraw-Hill.

Sanyal, B. C. (Ed.) (1983) *Higher Education and the New International Order: A Collection of Essays*. London: Pinter Publishers.

Seabury, P. (Ed.) (1975) *Universities in the Western World*. New York and London: The Free Press.

Simmons, A. and J. Q. Wilson (1980) Harvard's Revision: Two Views. *Dialogue*. Vol. 13:1.

Snow, C. P. (1963) *The Two Cultures: A Second Look*. London: Cambridge University Press.

Soedjatmoko (1985) The International Dimension of Universities in an Interdependent World. Address given to the 8th General Conference of the International Association of Universities, UCLA, August 12, 1985.

Teichler, U. (1983) Hochschule und Beschäftigungssystem. In: *Enzyklopädie Erziehungswissenschaft*. Vol. 10. Stuttgart: Klett Kotta.

Thompson, K. W., Fogel, B. R. and Danner, H. E. (1977) *Higher Education and Social Change*. New York: Praeger Publishers.

Trow, M. (1973) *Problems in the Transition from Elite to Mass Higher Education*. Berkeley: Carnegie Commission on Higher Education.

Weiler, H. (1984) Political Dilemma of Foreign Study. *Comparative Education Review*. Vol. 28:2 1984.

Western European Education (1976) Special Issue: *Mass Higher Education and the Elitist Tradition*. Vol. 1–2.